Understanding
English Surnames

Understanding English Surnames

SIR WILLIAM ADDISON

B. T. BATSFORD LTD
London

First published 1978
© Copyright Sir William Addison 1978

Photoset by Bristol Typesetting Co. Ltd,
Barton Manor, St. Philips, Bristol
Printed and bound in Great Britain by
Redwood Burn Ltd, Trowbridge & Esher
for the Publishers B. T. Batsford Ltd,
4 Fitzhardinge Street, London W1H 0AH

ISBN 0 7134 0565 1

Contents

Acknowledgements

Illustrations 3, 4, 6 and 7 are reproduced by permission of the Essex County Records Committee. They are examples of 'tell-tale' lists of local residents that may be consulted in any County Record Office. Pictures 1 and 2 are from L. Sewell, Long Melford, Suffolk. The author and publishers acknowledge their indebtedness.

List of Illustrations

Introduction

We have records in abundance of the names and achievements of our most eminent land-owning families. Only recently have we come to appreciate the extent to which in every county, and in some parts of the country in every parish, surnames are still to be found of families whose ancestors tilled the soil, shepherded the flocks, and drove the cattle for sale in the same market-towns for centuries, while their kinsmen trimmed the hedgerows that have contributed so much to the beauty of our English landscape. These 'others there were' are the people Gray had in mind when he wrote his *Elegy in a Country Churchyard.* Some laboured under compulsion from the lord of the manor, others as free tenants for the benefit of ·their children and their children's children; but whether by compulsion or freewill they established a way of life which continued unbroken until the Industrial Revolution disrupted it and produced a population without roots.

Only twice before had social disruption on such a scale been matched: first, when feudalism was imposed by the Normans; secondly, when the power of the Church was broken by the Tudors. Now, after two World Wars in a single generation have combined to produce economic and social chaos, thousands of people—the young no less than the old—are enquiring into the past, wanting to know whence they came in the hope that this will help them to understand what has happened and enable them to lay more secure foundations for the future. While frankly nostalgic, the instinct is by no means irrational. As the

Danish philosopher, Kierkegaard, said: 'History is lived forward, but is understood backward.'

The personal expression of this instinct is found in the rapidly developing interest in family history. People everywhere have acquired a new eagerness to know where their roots were and how their ancestors lived. And the first thing they learn is that as the study of a place starts with its name, the study of a family starts with its surname. It is the first clue to identity.

It has been estimated that there are at least one hundred thousand different surnames in daily use in the British Isles, of which not more than one-quarter have had their meaning satisfactorily explained. Fortunately for the amateur philologist there is an admirable *Dictionary of British Surnames* compiled by my old friend, Dr. P. H. Reaney, and it is the 'bible' from which many—perhaps most—of my 'texts' have been taken; but it deals with only between fifteen and twenty thousand. Obviously, some surnames do not require detailed examination. Their meaning is clear. A large proportion of these are either place-names or corruptions of place-names that call for study in groups rather than individually. Others, like Smith, which is probably held by as many as two hundred thousand separate families in England alone at the present time, do not provide much scope for speculation. Dr. Reaney requires only three words for its meaning: 'smith, blacksmith, farrier'. There does happen to be a place-name origin for a few of them; but apart from those the arguments do not arise from the meaning of the name but from the reasons for its frequency.

By contrast, the related name Marshall, from the Old French *mareschal*, which also means 'smith, blacksmith, farrier', has had an adventurous history. From an early date the farrier acted as vet, and when attached to a household he groomed the horses. This last duty resulted in the word 'groom' starting out on a romantic career associated with weddings, while the word 'marshall' not only became a surname, but from its humble origin developed into the name of the household officer who ordered the position of guests in the halls of castles and manor houses, until finally it attained the dignity of being the title borne by that high officer of state, the Earl Marshal. *The Boke of Curtasye* has the lines:

> *In halle marshalle alle men schalle sett,*
> *After their degre, withouten lett.*

Nor must we forget that farrier, 'worker in iron', gave us the name of the great Norman family that formerly held the earldom of Derby and estates from Bere Ferrers in Devon to Woodham Ferrers in Essex.

It was such reflections as these that suggested to me that there were other ways of looking at surnames, no less revealing than that of philology and equally valid. Some of these I have explored in this book.

The surname Marshall seemed a good starting point for such an exploration—or at least to justify it—because it reflects the importance of the horse at the time when surnames were being adopted. Palfreyman might also serve. It was the name borne by the man in charge of the palfreys, or saddle-horses—the groom, in fact, who attended the ladies of the household when they took the air on the Downs. And no Yorkshireman needs to be reminded of the regional significance of the horse.

But this, of course, is only one small group of surnames that have survived from the Age of Chivalry. Others introduce Sworder, Spurrier, Archer, Bowyer, Alabaster, each of which had its origin in the days of mediaeval honour and courtesy—the attribute that gave us the surname Curtis. An arbalestier was a crossbowman. One family of that name held land by serjeanty of serving with an arbalest at Wallingford Castle, another by guarding Exeter gaol. Then there were the falconers, who survive as Faulkner. In 1264 a man of that name paid one falcon's hood and one penny yearly for twenty-six acres of land at Walthamstow in Essex. The present-day Bachelors, or Batchelors, may fear that their remote ancestor was an unmarried man. The truth is that the original Bachelors were either young knights who followed the banner of a knight of higher rank—novices in arms—or junior members of a trade guild. The first meaning survives in the oldest Order of Knighthood, Knight Bachelor, the second in the first degree at a University. Child, or Childe, is a common survivor from the same Age. A Child in the thirteenth and fourteenth centuries was a young nobleman awaiting knighthood. In Malory's *Morte D'Arthur* there is a reference to a youth named Chastelayne, 'a chylde of the Kynges chambre', and Byron revived the use of the soubriquet in *Childe Harold.*

The recurrence of French elements in the oldest English surnames is due to their being introduced into this country by the Normans. Camden, the first English writer on the subject, says in *Remaines Concerning Britaine*: 'About the yeare of our Lord 1000 surnames began to be taken in France. But not in England till about the time of the Conquest, or else a little before, under King Edward the Confessor, who was all Frenchified'. But long before they became hereditary second names were coming into use as distinguishing tabs. They were then either nicknames or toponymics relating a man to his place of residence or origin. Like Topsy, surnames just grew. It is because they were never required to conform to strict rules that there is so much mythology about them.

In a sense, all surnames began as nicknames conferred for purposes of identification, and many of the oldest were far from being complimentary. So it is not surprising that some have been abandoned for more socially acceptable alternatives. On the other hand, there are names that began as compliments which in truncated form have become liabilities. A man born to bear the name Bumble might feel handicapped in life, and derive little comfort from having had it immortalised as that of a consequential, domineering parish official by Charles Dickens. He would be unlikely to know that Bumble is a contraction of *bon-bel*, 'good and beautiful'. *Bon-coeur* has suffered a similar fate and become Bunker; *Bonne-foy*, 'good faith', has become Boffey, or so the boffins tell us! Doubts, however, must frequently arise when we note the number of variants of even familiar names. Sir William Dugdale, the seventeenth-century Garter King of Arms, is alleged to have said that he had found one hundred and thirty different ways of spelling Mainwaring, and a persevering collector of the different ways of spelling Shakespeare might one day find a place in a *Book of Records*.

Different spellings can even confuse scholars over the origins of the simplest names. So, for that matter, can the same spelling. Seller, for example, may mean no more than dealer, even with the possessive 's' added. Sanson Sellarius of York, who was fined five marks in 1175 for selling shields to the king's enemies, was clearly a man who traded in shields, although his name would not at that date have become hereditary for a tradesman; but a certain Bodo Sellator of Suffolk turns out to have been a sadler. In the same county another source of the surname Sellers might be 'sealer of cloth', and yet another Master Sellers might have descended from the cellarer of St. Edmund's great abbey at Bury. The cellarer held an important office in monastic houses, although in this case the name was often changed to Taverner after the Dissolution of the Monasteries. As for John Seller of Sussex (1296), there is strong reason for believing that the 'sel' in his name meant 'shelter', and that he was the man who lived in the herdsman's hut on the Downs.

No doubt this confusion has deterred well-meaning legal experts from proposing the establishment of copyright in surnames. Many people are still surprised that there is .none—that a man can take any surname he pleases. The law remains precisely as it was when Lord Chelmsford (as he afterwards became) gave judgement in favour of the son of a female slave who had adopted the surname of her master and passed it on to her offspring. His lordship's words were: 'The mere assumption of a name which is the patronymic of a family by a stranger who had never before been called by that name, whatever cause of annoyance it may be to that family, is a grievance for which our law affords no redress'.

The most amazing venture into the realm of indiscriminately conferred surnames was the practice adopted by the governors of the Foundling Hospital in the middle of the eighteenth century. Clearly the foundlings in a Christian institution must be baptised, so on 29 March 1741 the first batch were duly received into the Church in the presence of many of the most exalted in the land, including the Duke of

Bedford, the Duke and Duchess of Richmond, and others of noble rank who graciously acted as sponsors and allowed the children to be given their names. As the result of this, the first register of the Foundling Hospital outshines that of the most aristocratic parish in the land. When the names of the nobility had been exhausted they were succeeded by a select list of Christian saints and martyrs, which in turn gave place to a sequence of poets, philosophers, generals, admirals, and novelists, who in turn opened up the field for fictional characters including, perhaps, the consequential Mr. Bumble. Finally, the governors turned to the limitless resources of the Natural Creation, which at least avoided the risk of a bad penny turning up at an ancestral home to claim relationship with the holder of a venerated title on the strength of his father's admission to the Foundling Hospital.

In 1761 an Act was passed by Parliament directing that all children brought into workhouses, whose names were unknown, should be given one by the overseers and church-wardens. Crabbe, in *The Parish Register*, tells us that in his town foundlings were named after the day of the week on which they were picked up. So, after hearing the circumstances of the discovery, the village elders

> *Next enquired the day when, passing by,*
> *Th' unlucky peasant heard the stranger cry.*
> *This known, how food and raiment they might give*
> *Was next debated, for the rogue would live.*
> *Back to their homes the prudent vestry went,*
> *And Richard Monday to the workhouse sent.*

No doubt it was considered an act of Christian charity when one such child was baptised Tom Amongus, because in the seventeenth century baptismal names could be far more cruel than surnames. At Waldron in Sussex an entry in the parish register reads: 'Flie-fornication, the bace sonne of Catren Andrewes, bapt. ye 17th Decemb. 1609'.

The more ribald of the surnames that survived into the Age of Dickens from the Age of Chaucer have now disappeared. The Brekewombs, Cachemaydes, Cachepenises, and Cuttepurses have either died out or taken other names.

It is not as a rule difficult to make a name look respectable. The Weatherheads may have started as Wetherheads (sheep's heads), the Bests as Beasts. Some nicknames may continue to be cherished. The descendant of the first butcher to be given the surname 'Hackbone' may continue to rejoice in it if he follows the same trade. Not infrequently the rub has come when the bearer of such a name has proposed marriage to a girl with a pleasanter name. Fortunately, some of these names are no longer suspected of meaning what they do. Few, for example, will know that Hollyer is said to be derived from the Old French word for whore-monger or fornicator. If a lady objects to names with apparent references to the rear extremities, such as Rams-bottom, Sidebottom, or Shufflebottom, it can, of course, be explained to her that these names are topographical, not anatomical.

Several names suggesting a bestial origin, including the surname we have just seen modified to Best, are derived from parts played by the original bearers in the old Miracle Plays that were so prominent a part of mediaeval village life. The number of such surnames is a constant source of surprise to beginners in the study of names. They preserve the record of a folk culture that official records might have passed by. For this, if for no other reason, the nicknames that survive are not to be scorned. Take the surname Drinkepin, for example. Surely it must refer to the large drinking vessels that had pegs fixed on the inside to indicate measure. It is from these that we get the phrase 'take him down a peg or two' for reducing a man's self-esteem.

Surnames conferred for official records fall into three main groups: occupation names, representing twelve to twenty *per cent* (according to region) of English surnames, patronymics, representing up to thirty *per cent*, and names derived from place-names, which account for considerably more than fifty *per cent* of all surnames. As a starting point for occupation names we cannot do better than go through the list of the Livery Companies of the City of London. The original Pothecary would be an apothecary, and the name survives in Hampshire, the county in which it appears to have been first corrupted to Potticary. After the Apothecaries in the alphabetical list come the Armourers, who gave us the Armers, Armours, and Larmours, and the Brazers, who produced the Braziers. The Bowyers may appear as Boyer, the Cordwainers as Cordner or even Codner. Sometimes family pronunciation of an occupation name provides a clue to its origin, as with Cowper from *couper*. Most of the variants were introduced, as we should expect, to shorten a name. In this way Fishmonger became Fisher and Farrier, Farrer. Surnames derived from crafts that were protected by the ancient guilds were basic: Fletcher, Horner, Salter, Skinner, Chandler, Turner, Vintner, and many others. The august five who take precedence provide their own commentary on City wealth. They are the Mercers, the Grocers, the Drapers, the Fishmongers, and the Goldsmiths.

Such ancient crafts as these continued to provide most of the occupation surnames not directly associated with the land until the fourteenth century, when Edward III brought over from Flanders weavers to expand the English cloth trade, which became the source of so much wealth in the Middle Ages. The various crafts, or misteries, associated with clothmaking produced a rich crop of surnames, which might vary from region to region, and in doing so provide clues to the place of origin of the families bearing them. Fuller is an example. It comes from the French *fouler*, 'to trample'. The object of the process was to thicken and whiten the cloth, and this was originally done by treading it out in a trough. In the West of England fullers were called Tucker, from an Old English word which meant 'to torment', and is closely related to *tāsion*, which means 'to toze, or tease'. So the fuller's, or tucker's, teasel gave us the surname Tozer, which suggests that anyone bearing it had ancestors connected with the cloth trade in Dorset or Somerset. In the Midlands and the North of England, on the principal that a a spade should be called a spade, a fuller might be called what in fact he was, a Walker. Wycliffe's translation of Mark ix,3 bears this out in the sentence: 'And his clothis ben maad schynynge and white ful moche as snow, and which maner clothis a *fullere*, or *walkere* of cloth may not make white on erthe'.

The mediaeval Clothiers became a new social class in the small towns of the West Country and East Anglia, where they took the place of the earlier Merchants of the Staple. They built churches, endowed almshouses, and when the trade became widely dispersed fulling was not the only craft to produce alternative surnames that provide clues to places of origin. The weavers themselves might be Webbers, Websters, or Webbs according to where they lived. The Webbs are found south of a line connecting the Dee with the Wash. They extend across a broad belt from Somerset in the West, through Wiltshire, the South Midlands, into East Anglia. Somerset, being a large county lying between the West Midlands and the far West of England, has pockets of surnames with particular histories, and we shall look at them later. At the moment we merely note the fact that in Somerset the Webbs are joined by the Weavers, who in Devonshire become Webbers. The name Weaver moves northward from Somerset into Gloucestershire and Worcestershire, while in Lancashire and Yorkshire, which since the Industrial Revolution have been thought of as the home of weaving, the mediaeval weavers were called Webster, which had originally been the female form of the name. Webster is still a common surname in the Industrial North, and one wonders how many of those who tend the looms today are descended from the Websters of the hand-loom weaving days. Few indeed will now claim descent from the weavers who bore the name celebrated in Ben Jonson's *Tale of a Tub* (iv.2): 'My godsire's name, I tell you, was *In-and-in-Shuttle*, and a weaver he was'.

Not all occupation names can be so neatly plotted. Baker, for example, which is often Baxter in East Anglia, is erratically distributed, with a tendency to cling to the south and east coasts for no apparent reason. Fry, from the Old English word for 'free', is curiously confined to the South and West Midlands, with Freeman as its counterpart in the North Midlands. Like Webb, it seldom crosses the line drawn from the Dee to the Wash. Perhaps a wag might be able to make out a case for the name being more specifically defined elsewhere, as in Freelove and Freebody.

Names ending in 'man' were usually held by servants; but the terminal was sometimes added to a place-name to indicate special responsibility for a manned post. Bridgeman, for example, would be the name given to the official who guarded a bridge or collected tolls. We never get Fordman early because fords were free; but we do get Yateman for the man who collected tolls at gates. Gate, however, has more than one meaning. In the South of England a gate may be a gap in a range of hills; in the North it may be a road. There are twenty 'gates' in the city of York alone. And this use of the word is by no means confined to the North, so in many parts of the country a man called Gates or Yates might be a roadmender.

When surnames were introduced, the first to assume them by right of heredity were landowners, who took the name of their estates in the way the Highland chiefs still do. Some of these were already held at the Conquest by a few land-owning families like the Ardens of Warwickshire and the Asshetons of Lancashire, who have continued to this day. Anyone who goes round England with an eye open for the names of such families will soon discover that the oldest are held by the gentry, not by the nobility. Not one of the barons who forced the hand of King John at Runnymede has a direct male descendant in the House of Lords today.

The most important sources for early names are Domesday Book, the Hundred Rolls, the Pipe Rolls, the Charter Rolls, the Fine Rolls, and the Subsidy Rolls. The Hundred Rolls have been extensively used because they contain lists of landowners and tenants; but away from the eastern counties their value is limited. In all the rolls the fewness of Saxon names is remarkable and shows how complete the Conquest was. In most parts of the country they are found only in the lists of under-tenants and cotters. Some, however, survive. When a distinguished actor using the professional name, William Mervyn, died in 1976 it must have surprised those who were accustomed to seeing him in such parts as those of benign dignitaries of the Church, or slightly eccentric aristocrats, to learn that his real name was Pickwoad.

The coming of the Normans had an astonishingly rapid effect on personal names. William, which we would expect to have been the one most reviled, quickly became the most popular. Then with the arrival of the monks from France the names of saints and martyrs began to replace those of pagan heroes, which had been calculated to inspire fear and compel submission to supernatural forces. Many of these new names have survived in strange variants. Mary survives as Marriott and Maryatt, Margaret as Margetts, Margetson, Meggs, Megson, and Moggs. The many pet forms of this name remind us that at one time it meant pearl and was a universal favourite. Wycliffe likens the kingdom of Heaven to 'Margarite'. Most Biblical names had such meanings when they were adopted as surnames, so may be said to have had symbolic significance, and to have been intended to counter-act the sinister powers represented by the pagan names they replaced. It was as though the missionaries went round the country proclaiming 'Not Wan, but Ann!' The new names that proved most popular were David (the well-beloved), Gabriel (hero of God), Michael (god-like), Peter (the rock), and the greatest favourite of all: John, which has a host of derivatives, including Jones, which must be the runner-up to Smith in the table of frequency, although it would be difficult to compile such a table in view of the extraordinary number of variants for other favourites. David, for example, has produced Davey, Davidson, Davis, Davies, Dawkes, Dawkins, Daws, Dawson, Day, Davitt, Dowson, Dowden, Dowling, and many others.

In rural areas pre-Christian superstitions lived on, and because the lore of trees is closely associated with primitive religion, tree names were common. These varied in con-formity with local traditions and racial settlement; but it was probably out of resistance to French domination that so many Old English names were taken in preference to their French counterparts. The oak gave us names beginning with 'Ac', the birch those beginning with 'Birk', and so forth. The incidence of such names in counties can be as revealing as that of 'holt', 'hurst' and 'shaw' elements in place-names. For example, because the alder grows well in marshy places, we get Alldritt, Aldred, and Naldrett in Sussex. Some trees, of course, were common everywhere. Most cottage gardens had an apple-tree, and as these provided valuable food for animals they were planted in open country and became local landmarks in Saxon times. In fact, the Saxon Chronicle describes the Battle of Hastings taking place 'at the hoary apple-tree'.

These tree names led the way to the adoption of an infinite number of toponymics. Like the governors of the Foundling Hospital, our forefathers discovered that the names of saints and martyrs were soon exhausted, and that the most fruitful source for the supply of surnames as identification tabs was the natural environment which five centuries earlier had yielded such a plentiful crop of place-names. So it came about that, as the old couplet has it,

> *In ford, in ham, in ley, in ton,*
> *The most of English surnames run.*

The first of these surnames derived from a place began with a preposition. Atte, the commonest, is now incorporated in such names as Attlee, Attwater, and Attwood; but has been dropped from most of the names to which it was formerly attached. By is incorporated in Bywater and Bygates, which is now usually abbreviated to Byatts. The three names, Noakes, Nelmes, and Nash are corruptions of atten-oaks, atten-elms, and atten-ash, leaving the intruded 'n' as a clue to the original home of the name, which was probably in the West Midlands. The addition of 'n' to 'atte' was particularly common in Worcestershire, while in the South of England the prefix 'atte' tended to be discarded in the fourteenth century and the suffix 'er' substituted to produce such names as Brooker, Fenner, Fielder, Grover, Laker, Stocker, and so on, with 'V' replacing 'F' in the South West as the initial letter of a name. In 1332 twenty *per cent* of local surnames had dropped their preposition in Surrey, against only seven *per cent* in Somerset and six *per cent* in Suffolk. These dialectical peculiarities suggest oral rather than written conferring of names, and are commonest where the influence of French clerks was weakest.

At the beginning there was little need for swineherds and ploughmen to have surnames. The workmen who did need them were those who moved from open country into the larger villages and towns in which they had no form of identity. Obviously, the most convenient way to label them was to add to their personal name the name of the parish from which they had come. The number of place-name surnames in a district thus became an accepted indication of either its early industrialisation or the size of a local religious Foundation. Throughout the period in which surnames were being acquired the wealth of the Church was increasing, until at the end of the period it had become the nation's largest employer of labour.

By the end of the thirteenth century the adoption of village names as surnames had practically ceased in the South of England. As population increased and division of labour became more clearly defined it was found more helpful to identify men according to their calling, if they had become established in one, and the rest either in relation to the part of the parish in which they lived or to their parents. So Taylors, Millers, Turners and, of course, Smiths became common, to be followed by the names given to itinerant traders, which at first tended to be of French origin in most parts of the country where names were recorded by French clerks. In this way, we got pedlers from *pied*, giving rise to the surname Pedder; but in the West Country they were called chappers from the Old English word and given the surname Chapman, and in the North East of England a Norse word produced Copeman. But everywhere the commonest ending for any trade name was 'er', which is simply an abbreviation of the Latin *-arius*.

It is this kind of relationship—topographical, racial, and dialectical—between surnames and their origins and variants that has been my own special interest. Under the title *Homes of Family Names in Great Britain* (1890), Henry Guppy, a retired naval surgeon, collected between five and six thousand names of farming families in England and Wales,

choosing farmers because they were the most settled section
of the community, and produced a detailed analysis of their
distribution in 600 pages of close print. But after Ekwall's
work on place-names and Reaney's on surnames much of
what he thought conclusive must be rejected as either
irrelevant or misleading. He did, however, extract from
public records useful information about names that had
been confined to one county for several hundreds of years,
even although they originated in a place-name in another
county. Clearly, as such families had intermarried with
neighbours over a long period the question of their place of
origin had become academic and racially irrelevant. What
he tells us about the Pelhams[1], for example, is more useful
for the purposes of local history than what Reaney says
about them. Guppy is often able to tell us how the founder of
a branch of such a family came to a county. Many came as
constables of important castles. No-one so far as I know has
fully explored the effect of patronage in this field. Such
dignitaries of the Church as the bishops of Durham had
enormous power and must have found lucrative employment on their vast estates for their kith and kin. How many
Bainbridges, for example, who are now so numerous in
Northumberland and Durham, are descended from kinsmen
of the great Christopher Bainbridge, bishop of Durham,
archbishop of York, and finally cardinal, who died in 1514?
Many such questions have come into my mind while
writing. But Guppy was right in taking the names of farming
families as the basis of his research, and I have used his lists
as my own starting point in many counties.

The field for such research can now be broadened from
that of the landed gentry to that of yeoman families—men
'whose limbs were made in England'. It is these who have
most enduringly stamped their image on the land they loved
and served, and have contributed to our national character
the stability and resolution that carries us through every
crisis. I hope that what I have written will stimulate those
who bear these regional names to re-establish relationship

1. See p. 26.

with the places from which they sprang, because, as Sir Arthur Bryant put it: 'The yeoman farmer, using the word in its broadest sense, is the common ancestor of nearly every Englishman', and the human animal, like every other, has a strong homing instinct.

Happily, the regional volumes of the English Place-Name Society are now being succeeded by an English Surnames series, planned with the object of exploring historical origins and geographical distribution. A National Dictionary of Surnames on genealogical principles is in sight, thanks to the generosity of Dr. Marc Fitch, who through the Marc Fitch Fund has established an English Surnames Survey in the University of Leicester. The first volumes must have whetted the appetites of many local historians as they did mine. Although the study of surnames can never be as fully scientific as that of place-names, if only because places stay put, persons don't, the methods by which they are examined can be. Some of my own findings will be dismissed by scholars—who, after all, are not notably charitable towards each other! I shall be satisfied if they only serve as pegs on which the scholars can hang their more reputable hats.

CHAPTER ONE

South-East England

As the Normans landed in Sussex and built castles to guard the route between London and France, we might expect Kent and Sussex to be the counties in which Norman ancestry would be most evident. In fact there are few families in either with pedigrees traceable to one of the Conqueror's followers. But this is less surprising than it might appear. When William partitioned England among his supporters he created a score of earldoms, not one of which survives. In any case, claims to Norman ancestry have been viewed with more suspicion in the South-East than in most parts of the kingdom since the exposure of false evidence in the Battle Abbey Roll. We now know that the monks who kept this record left spaces blank so that they could be filled later with the names of benefactors who, on being told that their name did not appear on the Roll, received a gentle intimation that the omission could be rectified for a suitably generous consideration. There is nothing new about the sale of honours.

Any reference to noble families in Kent and Sussex must immediately bring the Sackvilles of Knole and the Sidneys of Penshurst to mind. Others came as Constables of the great castles. The Fiennes were hereditary Constables of Dover for centuries. The Erpinghams came with the appointment as Constable of Dover Castle of Sir Thomas Erpingham, who was with Henry V at Agincourt and is commemorated in that moving exchange:

Henry: *A good soft pillow for that good white head*
Were better than a churlish turf of France,

to which Sir Thomas valiantly replied:

> *Not so, my liege; this lodging likes me better,*
> *Since I may say: now lie I like a king.*

The Percies were barons of Petworth long before they attained the earldom of Northumberland, and their descendants are still seated at Petworth. They came as Constables of Arundel Castle. The Pelhams, despite their Hertfordshire name, reached Sussex during the reign of Edward I as Constables of Pevensey Castle, and were eventually held in such high regard that their badge, the buckle, is seen on at least eleven of the county's churches and as a decoration on many iron chimney-backs in Sussex farmhouses.

The Shirleys, who were at Wiston until 1678, came from Warwickshire, as we are reminded in Shakespeare's lines:

> *Hold up thy head, vile Scot, or thou art like*
> *Never to hold it up again! The spirits*
> *Of valiant Shirley, Stafford, Blount are in my arms.*

The body of this particular Shirley was brought home for burial at Newark Priory, Surrey. Branches of the Sussex Shirleys settled at Preston, Chiddingly and Wivelsfield. At Wiston they were succeeded by the Gorings.

This was a region in which knightly families flourished as in few other parts of the kingdom: Caryll, Castedell, Culpepper, Bartelot, Lewknor, Farnfold, Lunford, Pierrepoint, Poyning, Poyntz, Wharbleton, and many others. Several are still there. Others remind us of the truth of Shirley's lines:

> *The glories of our blood and state*
> *Are shadows, not substantial things.*

The havoc played among noble and knightly families by the Wars of the Roses, the Reformation, and the Civil War of the seventeenth century is seen everywhere in Southern England. The Tudors knew that they could never be safe while private armies remained in the control of men who, while paying lip service to the New Order, secretly prayed for a return to the Old. At Blechingley in Surrey there is a sumptuous monument to Sir Thomas Cawarden, Master of the Revels to Henry VIII, who lived like a prince at Blechingley Palace with a hundred liveried servants to attend him and armour to put over four hundred men in the field. But not all the old families were liquidated. Dering, the name of a family seated at Surrenden Dering from the fifteenth century to 1928, is a Domesday name. The Twysdens, or Twisdens, were at East Malling for three hundred years, and before that at Goudhurst.

These families stood up to be counted on the Royalist side when civil war broke out in the middle of the seventeenth century. Among them were the Culpeppers, who have been in Kent and Sussex since the fourteenth century and bear one of the county's most interesting local names. It means spicer—one who culls or gathers pepper. Others on the Royalist side were Sir John Manny of Linton Place, Sir John Tufton of Leeds Castle, Sir Edward Filmer of East Sutton, and Sir William Boteler of Teston.

There were far more Kent and Sussex families on the other side. Of the one hundred and thirty-one men nominated to sit at Westminster, furnished with all the powers of a High Court to try Charles I, eleven were Sussex men and bearers of Sussex names: Pelham, Burrell, Gratwick, Morley, Stapley, Temple, Norton, Fagg, Cawley, Goffe, and Downes. Cawley, the leader of the Sussex regicides, was the son of a Chichester brewer, and has a monument to his memory in St. Andrew's Church. The Burrells have been a Sussex family since the end of the twelfth century. Their name is derived from the Old French word *burel*, 'reddish brown', which was the usual colour of a coarse woollen cloth woven in Sussex; but the family is chiefly associated with the county's iron industry. The Burrells were among the three or four leading ironmasters when the trade was at its most prosperous, and from these Burrell ironmasters are descended the families at Knepp Castle, West Grinstead, and Ockenden House, Cuckfield. Fagg has been a Kent and Sussex name since Domesday. A farm near Rye may have been the family's original home. These one-syllable names are common in all the southern counties. Digg and Digges have been common names in Kent since the time of Henry III. The most eminent member of the family, Sir Dudley Digges, has a fine monument at Chilham. As for the Days, it would be difficult to count them.

Although the names of the Conqueror's personal favourites died out in Kent and Sussex, with one or two exceptions, there is good reason for believing that surnames were acquired here earlier than in any other English county except Hampshire. It is what we might expect, having regard to its nearness to the Continent; but the most interesting evidence is in the large number of nicknames that survive as surnames—in Kent especially. The Coyfe, or Quaife, family must head the list, since they claim descent from a Coyfe who came over with the Conqueror and wore a hood instead of a helmet at Hastings. Hence the name. Scrope means crab, so must have been given to a man with a crab-like gait. Hogben means huck-bone, or haunch-bone, so is a word that must be related to knuckle, or huckle, which in the Craven district of Yorkshire means bent-bone and explains why a hump-backed man in the Skipton area is called 'huck-backed'. I suppose Cruikshank in Scotland is the opposite number of Hogben in Kent.

A curious name that has been held with justifiable pride for a very long period in Kent is Knatchbull. Brasses and sumptuous monuments at Mersham bear testimony to the family's dignity and estate, yet the first part of the name can only mean 'fell, or knock on the head', leading to the conclusion that the original holder of the name was a famous knacker! All honour to the family that kept the name unmodified! Modifications always beg questions. The Styles, for example, obviously got their name from 'stile', which is derived from the Old English word *stigol*, and this is also obviously the source of that other Kentish name, Stickle. How then do we explain so many of these names surviving side by side? Were the Styles more reputable than the Stickles, or *vice versa*?

Dr. Reaney has an interesting example of this kind of change. He tells us that Thomas Bourer, who was born at

East Grinstead in Sussex, adopted the name of Bowra when he set up in practice as a surgeon at Sevenoaks in Kent in the seventeenth century. The Sussex form of the name, with such variants as Borer, Bower, and Bowers, originated with Thomas *atte Boure*, who was M.P. for Horsham in the fourteenth century, and adopted the custom referred to in the introduction to this book of substituting 'er' for 'atte', the one at the end, the other at the beginning of the name.

This substitution of 'ra' for 'er' by an educated man seems curious because it was dialectical, but doubtless he had his reason. Such substitutions are common in Kent. They include 'd' for 'th', 'a' for 'o', and 'oi' for 'i' as in 'moine' for mine. In north Kent we get 'hirst' or 'hyrst' in names that in the south of the county would end in 'hurst'. The dialectical shortening of syllables is particularly confusing, and has foxed many experts. Everest, which is definitely a Kent surname, is probably 'Ever' from *eofor*, the Old English word for boar, added to yet another corruption of 'hurst'. Fortunately, local usage frequently provides a clue to the true meaning of a syllable that appears to be in doubt. For instance, the Kent and Sussex name Lade, or Ladds, is pronounced by the families bearing it in both forms in the way *Piers Plowman* indicates when he talks about making 'lordes of Laddes'. Without this authority it might be suggested that the name is derived from 'lade', the local word for a water-course.

In Kent and Essex the two letters 'v' and 'w' were long regarded as transposable, as we are reminded in the question put by the judge to the immortal Samuel, or Samivell, Weller or Veller, as to whether he spelt his name with a W or a V. 'That depends upon the taste and fancy of the speller, my lord', replied Sam, 'I never had occasion to spell it more than once or twice in my life, but I spells it with a V'.[1] Weller, a common name in Kent, was borne by Thomas Weller, who held Tonbridge Castle for Cromwell, and is further localised because it means 'salt-boiler', a calling that gave birth to another crop of coastal names, including the obvious Salter,

1. *Pickwick Papers*, ch. XXXIV

although with this it has to be said that it could equally well be given to a man who lived on the Saltings. This local substitution of 'er' for 'atte' led to a good deal of confusion as to whether such surnames had a topographical or an occupational origin. In some the meaning, fortunately, is clear enough. Croucher is obviously from cross, Hatcher from hatch, or gate, Walder from wood. Of occupation names that are well established in the South-East, we have the Furzers who cleared the furze, the Fellicks who cleared the woodlands, the Stubbers who dug out the roots of felled trees, and the Pallisers who made palings long before Trollope discovered them.

One of the most familiar toponymics in the South-East is Strode, with its variants Strood and Stroud, all of which mean 'dweller by marshy ground'. They have figured in the records of Kent since the beginning of the thirteenth century, and are now incorporated in that true marshland name, Strudwick—'the dairy farm on the marshes'. In Sussex, the liability of the valleys to flood has produced such names as Diplock, 'deep lake or stream'. Heath, which as no-one needs to be reminded is a Kentish name, becomes Hoath, Hoad, or Hoather in Sussex. A less easily recognisable toponymic outside Kent, its county of origin, is Nethersole, derived from the local custom of calling a pond a 'sole', and the same might be said of Overall and Overbury, which in Kent may not derive from 'over' in the sense of above, as they do elsewhere, but from the German *ofer*, 'the bank of a stream'. Many of these odd derivations must continue to be speculative. They arise from Kent's proximity to the Continent, which has meant that its dialect has been affected by several races introducing words of similar meaning. But in accounting for *ofer*, Sir Frank Stenton's contention that from an early date Kent had an elaborate culture closely related to that of the Frankish Rhineland may be relevant.

Cowdray, an honoured name in Kent, is usually said to be from *condraie*, 'hazel copse', but the patrician family of that name in Sussex derive it from Coudrai in France. The name that might be suspected of being related, Corderey, presents no problems. It means rope-walk. So the man who bore it originally was a rope-maker. Simmons, with its variants of Simonds, Symons, and Symonds, again look simple. Surely it is from the personal name, Simon, which was a common name modified in parts of the country in which Scandinavian influence was strong into something closer to the Old Norse *sigmundr*. In Kent, however, the discovery in the records of the Cinque Ports, under date 1294, that the good ship *De la Bochere* of Winchelsea was commanded by a certain Benedict Seman led to the suggestion that in the South-East Simon might be seaman, which conforms with the local habit of substituting 'i' for 'e' in the surname Sinnock, which like Sennock and Snooks, is a corruption of Sevenoaks. Simcock, however, is the one corrupted name in this group that must be allowed to have its source in Simon, since the addition of 'cock' to an abbreviated name is a very old familiarised form of surname, which lives on in the question often heard among countrymen: 'Watcher, cock?'

I frequently reflect on the wisdom of an old farm labourer who after listening to a trendy sermon in church whispered to me: 'The trouble with these eddicated types is they are so durned iggerant'. He, or his counterpart, might not know that the Durtnells or Dartnells, who have been in the Tunbridge Wells area since 1240 get their name from a lost place called Durkinhole in Leigh; but country folk can often put an enquirer on to local names for places that are only known by them. Claridge, for example, is from Claredge Wood in Waldron, Crittall from Crit Hall in Benenden, Goringe from Goring, and Henty from Antye Farm in Wivelsfield, to take a few names that are well-known nationally but have a narrowly local origin. Bedser and Pilbeam are two others that have their source in lost places, the memory of which can only live on in country lore.

The number of surnames derived from well-known place-names in Kent and Sussex is comparatively small. This is not, in fact, difficult to explain. When industries developed in these counties they were located in villages rather than in corporate towns, so nicknames, occupation names and toponymics were sufficient for purposes of identification. One of the oldest names in Kent must be Whatman, which is derived from an Old English word meaning 'bold, brave' and is typical of Saxon names as we shall find them in Hampshire. This fine old family farmed land near Romney and Hawkhurst for centuries, and will always be honoured for generous benefactions to the monastic houses of Kent. Eventually the name came to James Whatman, who in 1739 converted an old fulling-mill at Boxley into a paper-mill and made the name famous in an industry that had been introduced into the county by a German named Spielman during the reign of Elizabeth I, and is still associated with families in Kent whose members have distinguished themselves in public life.

Clothmaking developed early in the villages south-east of the Medway between Maidstone and Tonbridge, and east of that region through Brenchley (a distinguished surname in Kent) and Cranbrook, which in 1580 had a larger population than Maidstone, to a line linking Ashford with Tenterden. It gave us several local names. Three of the wealthiest clothiers were Thomas Davy and Robert Ovenden of Cranbrook, and Joseph Skeate of Tenterden. To the south of this region iron-working flourished. Then in 1561 Walloon, or Dutch, refugees introduced silk-weaving to Canterbury, and cloth-weaving and market-gardening to Sandwich, which explains the large number of names beginning with Van still to be found in east Kent. Many of these names were first held by makers of bays and says.

The silk industry of Canterbury, started by the Walloons, was further developed in the eighteenth century when Huguenot refugees poured in after the revocation of the Edict of Nantes, bringing a string of names that include Beauvoir, Durand, Cartier, Perrin, Petit, Picard, Minet (later common in Dover), Delannoy, Campredon, Devereux, Lavaure, Lernoult, and Monins, all of which now have anglicised variants. The craft names they introduced include Cowper (*couper*, maker of wooden casks), Sayer (one who assays or tests), and Verrier for glazier. Dilnot, an intriguing name found in Sandwich, looks like an old name for the ground-nut, which was the cyclamen of the Herbals. It seems to have been peculiar to Sandwich for a long period. Does this suggest that it was another name introduced by a Walloon gardener?

Surrey also had its clothiers. The Chaloners derived their name from *chaloun*, 'blanket', which in turn was derived from the earlier place of manufacture, Châlons-sur-Marne. As early as 1252 'Chalons of Guildford' were bought for the king's use at Winchester Fair. Godalming, Wonersh, and Farnham were all woolmaking towns. Among the Surrey woolmen were the Hookes, Chittys, Mellershes, Woods, Wests, Periors, Hackmans, Webhams, and Chaundlers. Many of these families put the money they made from selling cloth into land and achieved county status. Among the most distinguished were the Abbotts, a family that has produced a bishop of Salisbury, an Archbishop of Canterbury, and a Lord Mayor of London.

Glassmaking was an industry in all these southern counties in the East; but was most prominent in Surrey, where the Shorters (Schurterres), Ropleys, and Peytos were the leading families, and Guildford and Chiddingfold the leading centres; but the industry ended abruptly in 1615 when Parliament decided that the use of timber from the Weald to feed its furnaces was scandalously wasteful. Leather is another trade which gave Surrey a crop of surnames.

But the greatest of all the industries in all these counties was iron-making, which survived in Sussex until 1809. It gave its name to many places and left a heritage, not of slag heaps but of lovely hammer ponds and such fine master's houses as Rudyard Kipling's Batemans at Burwash. Among the surnames it produced are Bloomer, Blower, and Ashburner. The mass of iron that had to be passed twice through the fire was called a 'bloom' and the refining house a Bloomery, so the bloomer was the man in charge of the process, while the blower was obviously the man who worked the bellows in the smelting house. His name has been corrupted to Blore and Blow, just as Bloomer has been corrupted to Bloom. The ashburner prepared wood-ash for the bloomer and perhaps also for the glazier, who left the surname Glazier in the region. Bowdler there is some doubt about. He was probably the man who puddled clay.

The tile-hung cottages of Kent and Sussex provide a clue to another local name: Hillier or Hellier, another example of the interchangeable vowel. It is from the Old English word *helion* and means tiler, which explains why Wat Tyler is referred to in Thomas Walsingham's *Chronicon Angliae* as Walterus Helier. Other local names will probably be argued about to the end of time. I have a bee in my bonnet about Clinch, which Dr. Reaney associates with clench, a name given to elevated dry land near a fen. This might be right, having regard to the frequency of the name near Sittingbourne; but there is a place in Sussex called Clinch Green, which might suggest to others besides myself that Clinch was the name given to a clincher, or riveter—a man who clinched. Does this not suggest that Clinch could be a name given to a nail-maker?

Other names found in the region that raise questions as to their meaning are Furlonger and Rivers. The Furlonger family have been in business as butchers in Surrey for more than two hundred years; but the name is found in a Subsidy Roll for Sussex as early as 1327, and as the word 'furlong' carried the additional meanings of a division of an unenclosed field and the track for running a race, a furlonger could have been a famous winner of prizes in local races. It seems the most likely origin of the name. Rivers is even more puzzling. It appears first in a Subsidy Roll as *atte Revere*. The French clerk who recorded it would be unlikely to know about the local confusion between 'e' and 'i', and it is noticeable that where *rivere* is recorded with the meaning of river, it is always *de la Rivere* (*rivere* being Old French). The odds are, then, that the Rivers families of Kent and Sussex took their name from *yfer*, which means edge, and signifies that they lived near the brow or edge of a hill or cliff. If they had been in the north of England they would have been suspected of having started life with an inherited predisposition for cattle stealing—reavers!

The well-known Kentish name, Chiesman, with several variants, has been established in Lewisham in its familiar form since the reign of Henry VIII. In an earlier form, Baldwin le Chesmangere appeared in the Pipe Roll in 1186.

And the name, which is familiar on shop signs in Kent, may remind us that at one time every tradesman had his symbolic sign, one of which would be a cheese. Now only the pawnbroker's brass balls and the barber's pole remain, and they are becoming rare. In Tudor times a common sign was the rose, which suggests that while many who bear the name may be justified in claiming descent from a Norman family called Rohere, others may simply be descendants of the goodman who lived at the sign of the rose. In Sussex this has special significance in the surname Pluckrose, which is derived from land held by the annual rent of a rose. There is one such property on the edge of Ashdown Forest in the possession of the Duchy of Lancaster, which as late as the middle of the last century was held by this rental. When it was due, the reeve of the manor called and plucked a red rose from a bush in front of the house, stuck it in his buttonhole and walked off.

Kent and Sussex are fortunate in that they have produced several good diarists, whose records are as valuable to those who wish to study the fluctuating fortunes of yeomen as the diary of John Evelyn is for more scientific studies. The Stapley line of squires, who lived at Hickstead Place, kept journals and account books covering no less than one hundred and thirty-six years from 1607 to 1743. Such records as theirs give us the clearest insight we can obtain into the life of such Sussex families as those of Bax, Campion, Courthope, Dodson, Scutt, Hart, Whitpaine, and Marchant, all with fine traditions. Kent is pre-eminent as yeoman country:

> *A squire of Wales, a knight of Cales,*
> *And a laird of the North Countree;*
> *A yeoman of Kent, with his yearly rent,*
> *Will buy them out all three.*

Much of this prosperity is due to the custom of gavelkind inheritance, which continued in Kent alone among English counties until it was abolished by legislation in 1926. Under this system estates were split up at a death and divided equally among the children after provision had been made

35

for the widow. This meant that whereas elsewhere the eldest son inherited the landed estate and his brothers had either to be provided for separately or left to fend for themselves, in Kent several sons might inherit single farms, and with industry extend their holdings into neighbouring parishes. The challenge of a small estate led to intensive cultivation of the land once the woodland had been cleared from much of the Weald, and made Kent 'the garden of England'. It led also to the pride in possession which is characteristic of many Kentish families like the Blaxland squires of Blaxland and the Wickenden yeomen, who derived their name from Wickendene in Cowden and flourished from 1200 until 'ould mother Wickenden' died in 1626. The family then lingered on in reduced estate until the last of the line, Joan Wickenden, died in 1740 after receiving parish relief most of her life. But Joan had not lost her passion for possessions. She was found to have salted away £250, which after giving her a decent burial was spent on the restoration of the parish church of Cowden. The surname survives.

I never reflect on the history of Kent without feeling what a happy circumstance it was that one of its histories should have been written by a man who was so completely in harmony with its spirit as Edward Hasted was. His family may have come from Hanover originally; but generations of Hasteds had tilled the soil of Kent and carried its produce to market before Edward was born, even although they spelt their name in at least ten different ways, including the variations of 'Has' through a range of prefixes from the personal 'Hal', through 'Haye', suggesting an enclosure, to 'High'. Fortunately, an expert of the eminence of Professor Alan Everitt examined them in detail[1] and concluded that as the early distribution of the name was over a group of eight or nine parishes between Faversham, Sittingbourne, Hollingbourne, and Lenham, and as at least three of the forms indicate altitude, the most probable source of the name is a farm called Highsted.

This argument is strengthened by the discovery that a

---

1. Foreword to vol. II, *English Surnames Survey*

bearer of the name at the end of the twelfth century held a property of that name. The family continues to flourish. In 1975 there were twenty-four branches of the Hasted family represented in the Telephone Directories of the Canterbury and Tunbridge Wells areas. As the name is practically unknown away from the South-East it is a remarkable example of a family name confined to a single area continuing for at least eight hundred years.

Among place-names apparently unrelated to the county that have become prominent as surnames, Baldock is outstanding. It can only come from Baldock in Hertfordshire, yet there are more Baldocks in Kent than in the counties north of the Thames. It was probably introduced into Kent by a vicar of Reculver in 1594, and if this is so it is an interesting example of what in some counties might almost be described as colonisation by a clerical family. From Reculver the name spread to Aylesford at the end of the seventeenth century, to Canterbury in the eighteenth, and there are Baldock memorials at Lenham below the North Downs. Those who scan the lists of former rectors on the walls of parish churches will often see the name of a rector bearing an alien place-name, whose descendants are still leaders in local life. Local historians, at all events, do not need to be reminded of our indebtedness to the clergy in times when the Church of England, however much it may be criticised today, guaranteed an educated person to every parish in the land.

CHAPTER TWO
Wessex

Viscount Grey of Fallodon used to tell his friends how impressed Col. Roosevelt had been by the inscription on a Jacobean tomb at Tichborne in Hampshire, recording the wish of the commemorated to be buried in the church built by an ancestor five hundred years earlier. It is not only to an American that such a record gives a sense of security and steadfastness. What is even more gratifying is that in Hampshire the common people have a record establishing ancient lineage. One of the earliest lists of surnames in England is in a survey of the inhabitants of Winchester made in or about the actual year of the Conquest, twenty years before Domesday. Norman names, of course, appear in the list, as we should expect in view of Edward the Confessor's love of France and Winchester's status at that time. They include Durand, the name we found in the South-East, along with Allen, Austin, and Walter in their various forms, all of which are Norman, and the more distinctive Norman name, Finnemore, from *fin amour*.

For Austin, or Austen, we must have special regard in Hampshire since this was Jane's county. As the vernacular form of Augustine it was highly esteemed, and Walter, which rapidly became one of the most popular personal names, produced in FitzWalter one of our earliest patronymics. But it is the Old English personal names that are still current in the county, or at all events pre-Norman names, that give the list its special interest. They include Eldred, Elgar, Baldwin, Kemp or Camp, Collin, Goodrich, Halden, Lamb, Lewin, and Wade. Most of these are valiant names for any man to bear. Eldred, or Aldred, means 'old and noble counsel'; Baldwin, 'bold friend'; Kemp, 'warrior'; Goodrich, 'good or god ruler'; Lewin, 'beloved friend'; while Wade originated in the name of a sea-giant whose exploits were sung by minstrels long after most of the heroes of ancient song had been forgotten, and Lamb is a shortened form of Lambert, a saint greatly venerated in Flanders.

Most of the names noted in the South-East of England continue into the region we are calling for convenience Wessex; but with such dialectical changes as Fidler into Vidler, Fowler into Vowler, Fen into Venn, Folkes into Vokes, Seeley into Zealey, Seller into Zeller, and so on until we reach Dorset, where the Vs gain the upper hand universally and the Zs get the better of the Ss. Even so, as with Cowdray in the South-East, there are families claiming a more manorial origin, as when the Vidlers claim that their name is derived from *Vis-de-Leuu* (Wolf's face). Another curious feature is the intrusion of 'e' before 'a' as in Neame for Name.

As Norman influence was so strong in Hampshire even before the Conquest, it is not surprising that the custom of adopting Norman baptismal names, which spread so rapidly across the whole of England after the Conquest, should have started there. Even without that pre-Conquest connection with France, Normanisation would have been expected to show itself early as the result of sporting interests in the New Forest and the Church's vast estates in the county. Winchester records show that the decisive period was the first half of the twelfth century. Whereas in 1115 two out of every six children were given English names at baptism, in 1148 every child without exception received a French name, to many of which -son was added when personal names became hereditary as surnames. So the common belief that most surnames ending in -son are Northern is not valid for those adopted before the fourteenth century.

Many of the names found in the 1145 *Liber Wintoniensis* are now common in other counties; but a few are still most closely associated with Hampshire. They include Chute (which must have started in Wiltshire), Dummer, Free-mantle, Hursley, Lasham, Odham (from Odiham), and

Popham. The Vyne, a lovely Tudor house at Sherborne St. John, which for three hundred years was the home of the Chute family, is now in the care of the National Trust. The most famous bearer of the name was Chaloner Chute, Speaker of the House of Commons in Richard Cromwell's Parliament. His baptismal name, as we have seen, gives a clue to a source of family wealth. It was the great name in the manufacture of blankets.

The noticeable lack of any boundary line for surnames in east Hampshire is understandable in view of the lack of any sharply dividing topographical feature there—except, perhaps, the Hog's Back, which as a ridgeway can hardly be classed as a barrier. So we have the Wapshott family of Chertsey, which may be derived from de Hoppeshort. If so, the Chertsey family will probably be related to a Ralph de Hoppeshort, who held land at Beckhampton by serjeanty of keeping the king's harriers. In the west of the county the New Forest produced its more individualised crop of surnames. The place-name Lyndhurst is a reminder that at one time the lime was one of our commonest trees. Lyndhurst means 'lime, or linden, wood', and gave rise to such surnames as Lines, Lynes, Lind, Lindley, and Linley, with the reservation that while Lind-leah must mean lime-glade, Lin-leah could mean 'clearing where flax is grown'.

The Porcells in the New Forest were, as the name implies, swineherds, reminding us of the days when great herds of swine roamed through all our English forests. One of the most romantic of these New Forest names is Purkess, Purkiss, or Purchase, derived from an Old French word *purchas*, which meant 'pursuit or pillage'. A Purchase the Pursuivant was noted in the time of Henry VI; but the most interesting story connected with the name was told in a speech by Lord Palmerston, who lived at Romsey, and is now recorded on the Rufus Stone. It relates how a small estate near Stoney Cross had been in the possession of the Purkis family continuously since a lime-burner of that name was given it as a reward for picking up the body of Rufus and carrying it in his cart to Winchester.

But while Hampshire can claim to have established a surname pattern early, it has to be admitted that among its prouder families it was also lost early, although some of the great names will never be forgotten. We shall always be reminded of the Paulets at Basing in the monuments to William Paulet, 1st Marquess of Winchester, who died in 1571, and the 6th and last Duke of Bolton and 11th Marquess of Winchester, who died in 1794. The Wallops, whose original name of Barton was exchanged for a territorial name meaning 'valley of the stream', were Knights of the Shire from the reign of Edward III to that of Henry V and continued to dominate 'pocket boroughs' in the county until these were abolished. Nor can we forget the Oglanders of Nunwell, Isle of Wight, who were to continue in proud estate so long from the time when their ancestor, on landing with William at Hastings, undertook the subjection of the Isle, and finding it much to his liking settled there.

A fifteenth-century table tomb near the south porch of the church at Ellingham, on the Hampshire–Dorset border, is believed to be that of Sir Robert Punchardon, whose family were lords of the manor from the twelfth to the sixteenth century. After visiting this most lovingly tended of the five churches in the six miles between Fordingbridge and Ringwood a few years ago, I wandered into an antique shop in Fordingbridge and found the surname of a member of this ancient family on the flyleaf of a Bible, with a nineteenth-century date after it—evidence of a record of seven hundred years of this family on the banks of the Avon. Their name is found near Barnstaple in Heanton Punchardon, and at Thickley Punchardon in County Durham.

But these long-established families have been exceptions in Hampshire, despite the number of high-ranking Service personnel whose names figure in every local directory. The reason why so many Norman names disappeared early is that Hampshire has suffered two social Revolutions. The Church had brought the county's agriculture to a high level of prosperity when the Tudors came to the throne, and although it may be argued that little of this filtered through to the man who worked on the land, it has to be remembered that money counted for little in those self-supporting communities and that, on the whole, 'there was good living under the Crook'. The consequence of this advanced economy was that at the Dissolution the estates were parcelled out among Tudor favourites, who displaced most of the old Roman Catholic families. And when in the eighteenth and nineteenth centuries Industry replaced Agriculture as the source of sudden wealth, Hampshire got a third social structure which is reflected in the many new names that appear at that time in its parish registers.

After making due allowance for his habitual exaggeration, we may find that Cobbett was not very wide of the mark when he wrote of east Hampshire that during 'the short space of a hundred and thirty-one years, and, indeed, in the space of the last forty', more property had changed hands than during the previous seven hundred years, despite the Protestant Reformation. 'At Aldbury . . . Mr. Drummond (a banker) is in the seat of one of the Howards, and, close by, he has bought the estate, just pulled down the house, and blotted out the memory of the Godchalls'. Here he reminds us of an old South Country surname which was a corruption of 'good souls', so may be taken to be from the name 'Goodsoul', bestowed on an honest man as early as the twelfth century in Hampshire, where the kindred name, Godsell (God's hill), is found as both a surname and a place-name (Godshall) in the Isle of Wight. This name, however, is not confined to Hampshire. There are Godsell Farms in both Wiltshire and Sussex, and Gadshill, the home of Charles Dickens near Rochester may be from the same source. As a surname, Godsell now appears to have worked its way up into Worcestershire and Shropshire.

At Chilworth, Cobbett found that a powder-maker named Tinkler had got hold of the estate of the old Duchess of Marlborough. The interest in this name is that it is evidence of infiltration from the North of England. It is derived from tinker, metal worker, which in the Middle Ages was confined as Tinkler to Lancashire, Yorkshire, Cumberland and Northumberland. The intruded 'l' is probably due to the custom of tinkers announcing their presence by tinkling a bell.

A Mr. Laing had displaced the lineal descendants of Sir William Temple. Arlesford had lost the Gages, a Hampshire family name derived from the Old French *gauger*, exciseman. At Martyr's Worthy, the displacement of the Ogle family started another hare for Cobbett, who tells us that they had long been seated there. On looking into their record we find that they were a clerical family, supporting the point we made in Kent that parsons were great seed-carriers from one county to another. The Hampshire Ogles, who must have come originally from Ogle in Northumberland, contributed several dignitaries of the Church to the county of their adoption. Among other Hampshire parson families to produce fertile progeny in the county were the Garniers, the Poulters, the Norths, the De Grays, and the Haygarths. All were eighteenth-century pluralists. It is said that at one time the Norths held thirty livings.

But in Hampshire the bankers rather than the parsons made the grade, and Cobbett spoke a truer word than he knew when he said that the Barings were already the 'great men in Hampshire'. In their case, Church and Bank were happily combined in that they all descend from an eighteenth-century John Baring of Devonshire, the son of the minister of a Lutheran church at Bremen in Saxony. The two who first settled in Hampshire were the 1st Lord Ashburton and his brother, Sir Thomas Baring, sons of the founder of the Bank that bears their name.

In the church at Farley, connected with the Fox and Fox-Strangeways families, are memorials to a great intellectual family associated with all the counties grouped together here as Wessex, the St. Johns. Henry St. John, 1st Viscount Bolingbroke (1678–1751), sat in Parliament for the family borough of Wootton Bassett in Wiltshire and was later Member for Berkshire. His nephew, John St. John, sat for Newport, Isle of Wight; Oliver St. John, 1st Viscount Grandison, was M.P. for Portsmouth.

Most of the names so far mentioned do not allow for much dispute about origins. One that does is Whitcher, the name of a respected yeoman and landowning family in the Winchester district for at least three hundred years. The

immediate reaction of laymen in philology on meeting the
name there would be that it is a corruption of Winchester.
But the experts will have no such simple solution. Guppy,
whose own name belongs to Dorset, says in *Homes of Family
Names*, that as it first appeared in the records he had
examined as Whityers it must mean 'wheatears'. Reaney
found it first in 1288 as Wiccher, and in 1333 as *le Whicchere*,
which appears to be strong evidence of an occupation origin.
There is an Old English word *hwicce*, 'chest', so the original
Whitcher may have been a maker of chests. Alternatively,
the name could signify 'dairy farmer'; Wicker would then
be related to Wickens, which has that meaning, and 'Wh'
and 'W' are interchangeable in many parts of England.

Another Hampshire name we might argue about is Poore,
originally appearing as *Le Pohier*, which would mean 'the
Picard', but it could also be from 'power', and even 'poor' is
not to be ruled out entirely. Anyway, it was pleasant to find
an epitaph in St. Bartholomew Hyde at Winchester to
Robert Poore, who died in 1640:

> *Let men detracte,*
> *Say what they can,*
> *Hee livd and dyed*
> *An honest man.*

On seeing this I was reminded of a memorial to Sir John
Strange, an eighteenth-century Master of the Rolls, in the
parish church at Leyton in Essex: 'an honest lawyer'. 'That's
Strange!' commented a visitor.

Two simple and long-established Hampshire surnames
are Stride and Budd. There was a Stride at Fawley in 1340,
and there have been Strides in the neighbourhood ever
since. The Budds have an equally long pedigree in Hampshire, although the name appeared early—probably as a
nickname—in both Oxfordshire and Somerset. The Budds
were well-to-do in Winchester in the seventeenth century,
serving in the office of mayor and making bequests to the
poor. What is noticeable is that these long-continuing names
are more frequently found in the west of the county than in
the east, and some have dialectical connotation. Moggs is a

good example. It is common in the Lymington area as the South of England counterpart of Meggs or Maggs, the possessive form of the pet name for Margaret. Similarly Rugg is found for 'ridge', which in the North of England would be Rigg. The most renowned member of the Mogg family was 'Molly Mogg', the 'fair maid' of the Rose Inn at Wokingham, who died in 1766.

The fickleness that Cobbett noted in the east of Hampshire is even more pronounced in Berkshire. 'The lands of Berkshire', wrote Thomas Fuller, 'are very skittish, and often cast their owners'. Guppy says that he found few survivors of surnames that had been common in Tudor and Stuart times. It is certainly true that few of the families mentioned in Ashmole's history of the county are still there. Many are fully extinct. Even the old yeoman families seem to have disappeared, with a few exceptions like Kimber, still found in Newbury, where John Kimber built a row of almshouses, and Gunter, which has been a Berkshire name since the thirteenth century.

Most of the old Berkshire surnames: Aldworth, Appleford, Chieveley, Ilsley, Inkpen (Ingpen), Lambourn, Pusey, Radley, Tidmarsh, and Wadley, are place-names. The Berkshire surname Ilsley is a corruption of Hildesley. Although two names that are common in the county, Longworth and Chilton, are found elsewhere, it may be accepted that most of the South Country Longworths originate in the Berkshire place of that name. The Aldworths were lords of the manor of Aldworth on the chalk downs, succeeding the Norman de la Beche family, who built the castle and are commemorated in the effigies in the parish church. The Puseys are especially interesting: they claim to have settled in the place of that name before the Conquest, and to have held the estate by cornage: the service of sounding a horn. Local tradition expands on this by maintaining that the place got its name from William Pewse, who received it for disclosing a plot against the life of Canute. What is certain is that the family became extinct in the male line in 1710; but that the horn is believed to have survived, and one of an ox, mounted on two hound's feet, with a silver-gilt ring round it bearing an inscription, is exhibited as the original. The weakness in the claim is that the inscription is clearly of fifteenth-century date; but it could, of course, have replaced an earlier one, or it could well have been that before the fifteenth century no-one would have questioned the horn's authenticity.

One of the best authenticated surnames surviving in Berkshire is Norris, a name derived from Hampstead Norris, a village north-east of Newbury which got the second part of its name from John Norreys, to whom it was sold in 1450. Sir William Norris, or Norreys, raised forces to depose Richard III, and the name continued to figure prominently until it appeared in a list of owners of swans on the Thames in the reign of James I, in which Lord Norreys is shown as the owner of swans at Bray, Wytham, and Yattendon. Other owners were Sir Thomas Englefield, Sir John and Sir Thomas Fettiplace, Sir John Forster of Aldermaston, Sir John Golafre of Fyfield, Sir John Kentwood of Childrey, and Sir Francis Knollys. This impressive list need not surprise us since Berkshire has Windsor as its crowning glory and was therefore court country, with Sir Francis Walsingham at Englefield, Lord Knollys at Caversham, and Sir Thomas Hoby at Bisham. Fettiplace and Golafre are the two curious names in the list. The former, although an Oxford name, was associated with Longworth, and Golafre had been associated with Fyfield since Sir John Golafre built the church and manor house there in the fourteenth century.

Windsor's presence may not have been entirely beneficial to the county. It may even have contributed to the disappearance of old and honoured names following James I's persecution of Roman Catholics. Many Berkshire families suffered at his hands, including the Eystons of East Hendred, who were related to Sir Thomas More.

Another record that provides evidence of the unsettled social structure of Berkshire is that of the labourers engaged when Reading Abbey was demolished, and equally that of those who bought lots. Both contain a greater range of names than might be expected at the time.

When we reach Wiltshire, which has the extraordinary distinction as a surname of being spelt in at least seventeen different ways, we find more names of British, or Celtic, origin than in any of the counties already looked at. Their survival is a reminder that when the invaders came into the region the natives took to the hills, and there held out until they were accepted by the new rulers. In Wiltshire they were also able to hold out in the valleys that run down from the ridgeways—largely, no doubt, because in the early Saxon period Wiltshire was a region of transit rather than of settlement, so these small settlements were bypassed. The effect of this has been to give the county a large proportion of names derived from the three topographical features that retained British names: hills, woods and streams. Calne, which is now a town on the banks of the Abberd brook, was originally the name of the stream; but in that case the British name was not retained for a surname as in most cases it was. Deverill is a British, or Welsh, river name; Melchet a forest name in which the first element is the Welsh *moel*, 'bare', the second is either the British *cēto*, or Welsh *coed*, 'wood'. Chute is from the same source, so is related. Among Wiltshire river-names that gave us a number of surnames is Winterbourne, the word for a stream that ran only in winter when the water table rose to a certain height. It is found in Dorset and Berkshire as well as Wiltshire.

For some reason difficult to discover, hill names are more likely to survive as surnames than either woodland or river names. So we get Clarendon, and Draycot in Draycot Cerne, in which the second part of the name may be derived from the Cerne family of Dorset. As this place lies south of a steep hill the 'Dray' in it may come from *draeg*, which means 'draw or drag' and survives in the phrase 'it's a bit of a drag' for something that requires unrewarding effort. 'Pen', which means hill in most places may mean enclosure, or simply pen, in Wiltshire. This would be perfectly understandable in this exceptionally exposed county, where shelter for both man and beast would be welcomed during inclement weather. There are also several places in Wiltshire meaning 'cold cots', giving rise to such local surnames as Caldecott,

Chalcot, Calcut, with at least twenty variants. These -cott terminals continue into Somerset and Devonshire.

On the whole, it is not the adoption of topographical place-names as surnames that is worthy of remark in Wiltshire, but that so many of them are better known as titles than as family names. We may think of Clarendon, Salisbury, Wilton, Avon, and many more. Survivals of Saxon names derived from place-names are found; but few of them end in the typical early Saxon suffixes: -ham, -ing, or even -ton. Edington might be cited as an exception. It is a place-name that produced a fairly common surname, and was the name of a fourteenth-century bishop of Winchester. Bonham could be mistaken for another; but it is, in fact, *bon homme*. Incidentally, there is a monument to a man with that name at Edington. But most Wiltshire surnames ending in Saxon suffixes are late. They include Bousfield, Brinkworth, Dauntsey, Farleigh, Keevil, Hursted, and Wicksted. Of these, Farleigh is found in several other counties. One old name that is indisputably Wiltshire, although now common in Berkshire and Dorset, is Baverstock, from the place of that name.

There are few, if any, names in Wiltshire with Scandinavian elements in them that go back to the time of the invasions, and although French names are common they are less so than in the counties to the south and west. Apart from those incorporated in compound place-names we find Bissett, Chamberlayne, Gurston, Pinkney, Rolleston, Kellaway (from Caillouet), and Cotterell. Goddard has already been mentioned as a name that has been found in the southern counties at least since the Conquest. It means 'God, or good hard', which may be thought not inappropriate as the name of a great Lord Chief Justice of our own day who tended to agree with Shakespeare that 'nothing emboldens sin so much as mercy'. It is found throughout Wessex. Jesus College at Bray was founded by William Goddard in 1609. The family has been represented at Upham and Swindon since the fifteenth century, and there are monuments to Goddards at Ogbourne St. Andrews, Aldbourne, and Ogbourne St. George, while at Winchester the name is honoured as that of a great headmaster. Other early Wiltshire names are Harding, Gunner, and Earwaker—pronounced Errica, which means 'ever watchful'.

But it is when we look at place-names in Wiltshire specifically to discover how many of them we can recognise, albeit in corrupted form, as surnames that we are impressed by the feudal character of the county. It is an impression that builds up as we move into Dorset, and from Dorset into Somerset and Devon; but as we travel westward through the southern counties it is in Wiltshire that we first encounter it in strength in such names as Alton Barnes, which takes us back to the Berners family remembered at St. Albans in Hertfordshire and Berners Roding in Essex. At Ashton Gifford and Broughton Gifford we are reminded of one of the greatest of all West Country families.

Some of these Wiltshire names have hidden snares for the unwary. In Chilton Foliat we have a word that could simply mean trap; but is, in fact, from *folie*, 'folly', which is an element remarkably common in Wiltshire and Warwickshire place-names, and not uncommon in surnames, including Foolé, Folley, and Follitts in Wiltshire. It was introduced by Sanson Foliot, who held Chilton Foliat, as we now spell the name, in 1236. Other feudal compound names with a Wiltshire family name incorporated include Cliffe Pypard, held by Clive Pipard in 1231, Collingbourne Ducis, held by Richard Douce in 1402—the name that gave us Dowsett, 'pleasing, agreeable', with the diminutive 'ett' tacked on to the end of it. The Dunsterville family were at Castle Combe in the thirteenth century.

The Thynnes of Longleat, a branch of the Botfield or Boteville family of Church Stretton in Shropshire, are said to have got their surname by describing themselves as 'of the Inn'. In support of what on the face of it sounds an unlikely origin it is maintained that their ancestor, John de Boteville, resided at one of the Inns of Court. Be that as it may, the interest in their name for many is that its spelling preserves the late Middle English peculiarity of doubling consonants and adding a final 'e', which we get again in Wyllie.

The Dissolution of the Monasteries brought a new crop of

surnames, and a new crop of legends, like the familiar one about the Horners and the Nursery Rhyme, *Little Jack Horner*, who pulled out a plum. In his *Brief Lives*, Aubrey quotes an old rhyme:

> *Hopton, Horner, Smyth, Knocknaile and Thynne,*
> *When Abbots went out, they came in.*

The disruption was less revolutionary in our next county, Dorset, than in most. Dorset is pre-eminently the county of long family memories. The Welds of East Lulworth claim descent from Edric, whose brother Alfric married King Ethelred's daughter. The Martyns, still eminent in the county, continued despite the Reformation to hold on to Puddletown, where they had lived since their ancestor, Martyn de Tours, came over with the Conqueror. The tenacity of the Strodes of Beaminster, the Clavells of Kimmeridge and Church Knowle, the Binghams, Bonds, Moygnes of Overmoigne and many others helps us to understand how Hardy came to be haunted by Time, and to feel in his bones that the only true test is the test of History. A member of the Bingham family was the Parson Tringham of *Tess of the D'Urbervilles*, which must now be the representative Dorset family to millions. It was he who told Durbeyfield that he was really Sir John D'Urberville, and visitors still file past the canopied tombs of the family in the church at Bere Regis with Hardy's description in mind: 'Their carvings defaced and broken, their brasses torn from their matrices, the rivet holes remaining like martin holes in a sand cliff'.

The D'Urbervilles were real enough no matter how they spelt their name. One member of the family, James Turberville, was Bishop of Exeter. We may wonder whether he knew that this proud name really meant 'trouble field'! Hardy is inescapable in Dorset whatever the subject of enquiry may be. *Under the Greenwood Tree* starts with 'The Tranter's Party' and we learn that in Wessex a tranter was a carrier, a word derived from the same source as transport. It lives on in a surname, and the Tranters and Gabriel Oaks are as reminiscent of the spirit of Dorset as the proudest of the

Turbervilles or D'Urbervilles. The country folk of Dorset have a spirit of belonging that we do not find in such strength in the Home Counties. The oldest families are all rooted in the soil. In the halls no less than in the cottages the talk is of weather, crops and livestock. Notable among them are the Hoopers, one of whom drank with Charles II in the cellar of the family home, and the story goes that the king was so enlivened by his wit and loyalty that he knighted him among the barrels. The Hardys themselves, among whom was Nelson's captain, Thomas Masterman Hardy, farmed Dorset land for centuries. Nor was Hardy alone among the great Victorians in having long Dorset ancestry. The Brownings have been in the county for five hundred years.

The production of strong individual character that sometimes flowers in genius and often in eccentricity in Dorset must to some extent be the result of inbreeding. Sometimes, perhaps, local loyalty has been over-tolerant of local 'characters'. Dorset J.P.s do not like to be reminded that Hutchins, the county's historian, wrote of William Freke of Hinton St. Mary, who died in 1744, that 'his understanding was deranged, but he acted as a Justice of the Peace many years'.

A name that has its real home in Dorset, but turns up in other southern counties is Scutt, which according to tradition is not a form of Scott, but from the tail of the hare, and was given as a nickname to one who could have sung with Wilfrid Scawen Blunt,

> *I like the hunting of the hare*
> *Better than that of the fox.*

It was a name borne by eleven mayors of Poole from 1621 to 1742. Others have given it a more sinister origin. They have derived it from the Old French word for a spy.

CHAPTER THREE
South-West England

The Quantock villages north-west of Taunton yield a fine crop of family names with pedigrees comparable with those of Dorset. The small village of Dodington, near Nether Stowey, was the home of a family that took its name from the place and flourished there from the reign of Henry II to that of George III, with a short break under Cromwell, when Sir Francis Dodington, king's Commissioner of Array and Colonel of Horse in the West under Charles I, had his estates confiscated and was reduced to maintaining himself as a working cutler in Paris until the Restoration. According to a tradition in the family, the estate passed from the normal line of descent as the result of an incident that occurred while one of the Dodingtons was instructing a solicitor drafting his will. According to the story, at the end of the session the solicitor was asked if he knew of any other members of the family who should be included in the entail. When he replied that he could think of none, a child playing in the corner of the room called out: 'Put me in!' 'That I will, my little fellow', exclaimed Mr. Dodington, with a laugh; 'but I don't think it will do you any good'. The boy's name was added and his descendants got the estate.

East Quantoxhead has been held by only two families since Domesday: the Paynels from 1086 to 1207, and since then by the Luttrells of Dunster, whose ancestor, Sir Geoffrey Luttrell, married the Paynel heiress. A nineteenth-century Luttrell was rector of the parish for seventy years. Their name is a diminutive of *loutre*, 'otter'. The Malet family of Washford, who gave their name to Shepton Mallet, claim descent from the Norman favourite who had the duty of burying King Harold. Other Quantock manorial families are St. Albyn of Alfoxton, Crosse of Thurloxton and Broomfield, Stawell, and Warre. Sir John Stawell, whose sumptuous monument is to be seen at Cothelstone, was a Royalist who paid a heavy price for his loyalty; but his son was recompensed with a peerage by Charles II. In Taunton itself we are reminded of the martyrs of the Monmouth Rebellion, many of whose names are still found in Somerset towns and villages.

South of the Vale of Taunton Deane, at the foot of the Blackdown Hills is Sampford Arundel, a place-name perpetuated in the surnames Arundel and Arundale, now too commonly attributed to Arundel in Sussex. The names start in the twelfth century in Dorset and Somerset, where the first recorded holder was Roger Arundel, Domesday tenant-in-chief of Sampford Arundel. Later it became much more eminent in Cornwall, where it is spelt Arundell, and is borne by three branches, seated respectively at Lanherne, Trerice, and Tolverne, all of which have produced men of distinction. The original Arundell settlement in Cornwall was at Lanherne. Sir John of Lanherne, a naval commander, died when caught in a storm in 1379 after repulsing the French off the Cornish coast. Another John of Lanherne (d. 1504) was bishop of Exeter. Sir John of Trerice (1495–1561), Vice-Admiral of the West, was known to Henry VIII, to whom he was an esquire of the body, as Jack of Tilbury. His grandson sat for several Cornish constituencies, and another Arundell, popularly known as Jack for the King, was compelled to surrender Pendennis Castle to Fairfax in 1646. Like the Stawells, the Arundells were rewarded for their loyalty with a peerage at the Restoration.

The Mendips are more remarkable for their occupation names than for their patrician names. These originated in the West in the lead mines which had attracted the Phoenicians to Cornwall long before surnames were adopted. Buddle, which has the characteristic substitution of 'u' for 'i', has been a Somerset name since the fourteenth century and is connected in the Mendips with lead-smelting. It was the name of the man who washed the ore. Vanner, which as

Fanner may simply mean winnower in some parts of the country, definitely comes into the same category as Buddle in Somerset because it was the name given to the man who tossed the pounded stone into the air so that the wind could fan it: that is to say, blow through it to clear away the light dust, leaving the ore on the shovel. It must not, however, be confused with Vennor, huntsman.

In the surnames Kiddle and Kidwell, curiously enough, we have 'i' substituted for 'o' in a name corrupted from 'cold well', the name that as Cadwell was borne by Arviragus, one of the king's sons in *Cymbeline*, while he lived in the woods. This is only one instance of many that could be found to illustrate the danger of playing the 'seek the letter game', which can be such fun, and is usually rewarding when related to place-names that become corrupted as surnames. In Somerset, for example, the Yorkshire substitution of 't' for 'd' is reversed in Biddlescombe from Bittiscombe, Kidner from Kitnor, and the enthusiastic intrusion of a 'd' in Holdford from Holford.

Surnames derived from the mediaeval wool trade appear in surprising variety in Somerset, reflecting, no doubt, the geographical situation of the county between the far West of England and the West Midlands. Clothier is still a common surname north of the Mendips; but when we turn to subsidiary crafts we find that whereas in Devonshire weavers are called Webber, fullers Tucker, and dyers simply Dyer, in Somerset weavers may be Webb, Webber, or even plain Weaver, and tuckers, despite the place-name Tuckerton, 'the town of the tuckers', continue to be called Fuller in some parts. Teaslers, who took their craft name from an Old English word meaning 'to tease', because they scratched the surface of the cloth with the dried heads of teasles, or 'fullers' thistles', produced the Somerset surnames Tozer, Toswell, Tosewell, and Tazewell, and later Comer, the man who combed. The 'z' in these names is, of course, entirely appropriate in the region in which,

> *The zweetest girl I ever zaw*
> *Was zucking zider through a ztraw.*

In the church at Croscombe—in Fortescue country—is a two-storeyed vestry in which the seven guilds of the place met. Among them were Webbers, Archers, Fullers, and so on, along with some with less familiar names, like Hugglers, who were probably day labourers, and if so may remind us that casual labour tended to be given different labels in different parts of the country. In Devonshire a herdsman hired by the day was called a dayman, and in view of the number of surnames that appear to be derived from the word we may think it must have been a common way of hiring labour there. They include Diamont, Dyment, and Dymont, in which we have a 't' excresence, whereas in Diamond and Daymond's Hill, Tiverton, which may have the same derivation, we have an added 'd'. For a herdsman the usual Somerset surname was Horder; for a harvest labourer, Coker.

Trade surnames have changed greatly over the years. A tailor might be called Cissore in the West of England (from scissors), a baker Pistore (pastry), a brewer Brasher or Bracer, a fidler Crowther. Whereas in the East and South of England a tanner was probably called Barker, from the name originally given to the man who collected the bark of trees used in the process of tanning, in the West of England Master Barker was probably a shepherd, from the Old French word *berker*, while a tanner was either called Tanner or Corour, which meant a dresser of leather, which he sold to Master Clouter, the cobbler.

When we turn to toponymics we can hardly be surprised to find a group of names derived from rivers or streams. As elsewhere they are British, or Welsh. Craddock is a Devonshire name derived from a Breton word related to the Welsh Cardog, the name of a Welsh prince, and the initial 'Y', which is common in the West, may sometimes be 'Ea', the Old English word for river. The surnames Yea and Yeo probably mean 'dweller by a stream'; but there is need for caution here because Yelland, another Devonshire surname, probably means 'dweller by the old cultivated land', while Youldon means 'dweller on the old hill'. Cary, the commonest of the West Country names derived from rivers, means 'pleasant stream' and is found as both a place-name and surname in many parts of England. The patrician Cary family assumed the variant Carew. Richard Carew (1555–1620), the county historian, who lived on the family estate at Anthony in Cornwall was of this family. So was that colourful bearer of the name, Bamfylde Moore Carew (1693–1770), the son of a parson, who joined the gipsies after running away from Tiverton School. Early in the nineteenth century Anthony passed to the Poles, and was held until 1961, when Sir John Carew Pole, Lord Lieutenant of Cornwall, conveyed it to the National Trust. The family continue to honour the true derivation of their name by pronouncing it 'Cary Poole'.

Other streams that have given rise to surnames in this region are Chew, Coker, Parret, and Cory, which is an old name for the River Lyd and lives on in Coryton. Its counterpart in Somerset is Curry, the old name of the stream that runs through Curry Malet, Curry Rivel, and East and West Curry. Two curious Somerset surnames with a watery origin are Bythesea and Bytheway. Bythesea means 'by the watercourse or drain', incorporating an element that comes from *sēogh* and is found in the names of a group of villages inland from Bridgwater towards Ilminster, where it means 'dweller by the lake or pool', reminding us of the time when much of Somerset was under water during the winter months, hence the county name, which means 'the summer dwellers' from *Somersaetas*. Needless to say, so unusual a name as Bythesea (pronounced Bithersey) has been given other derivations. One family bearing it maintain that they got it from an ancestor who was a foundling picked up on the seashore. And, incidentally, another family bearing a local surname credited, or debited, with foundling origin, Case, claim that three hundred years ago their ancestor was found on the doorstep of a gentleman who was alleged to be the father. He disclaimed paternity, but took the child in and gave it the surname as a reminder of the packing-case in which it was discovered.

In travelling through Somerset or Dorset we become increasingly aware of names seldom, if ever, found elsewhere in England, and when we reach Devonshire and Cornwall

57

the proportion increases until it must reach nearly half. Not only are so many of these West Country names confined to the area, they are different in character. For example, there are hardly any patronymics in Devon and Cornwall. In fact, the proportion is so small that in the Devonshire Subsidy Rolls not more than one surname in a thousand ends in -son, and most of those that do appear were already hereditary when they reached the county. Fitzpaine, 'son of pagan', is Norman; Hobson is a common early patronymic found across the whole of southern and eastern England, while Luveson, which might be thought an exception, is probably a corruption of the personal name Leofsuna. This lack of patronymics might be surprising to those who regard the Cornish as closely akin to the Welsh, with whom practically all surnames are patronymics. Another notable feature is that there are few 'burg' endings in either place-names or surnames in Devon, which points to the peaceful settlement of the county, rather than conquest by force of arms. An exception is 'berry' in Berry Head and Berry Pomeroy, which is corruption of *burh*.

This idiosyncratic character of the West Country in its adoption of surnames means that there are factors that we need to come to terms with if we are to differentiate rationally. This, no doubt, was only to be expected in view of the mixture of British, Breton, Celtic, and Norman elements co-existing. Gorrell, a surname common in North Devon, is an example of one in which location is important in determining meaning. It may be from the Old French *gorel*, 'pig', from the Old English *gārwulf*, 'spear-wolf', or simply be the name given to a man who lived near a muddy spring or well. In Worcestershire, where the name is also common, it is most likely to be from the Old English; in Devonshire it is almost certainly an abridgement of Gorwell, 'muddy spring or well'. Similarly, the apparently simple surname Yard, or Yarde, has more than one meaning. In the West of England it does not mean what it would mean in the North; but is from the Old English *gerd, gyrd*, 'virgate, thirty acres', and was given to a man who cultivated that measure of land.

Beadle is another name that we need to relate to its location. It is remarkably common in the West Country and takes a variety of forms, each of which may be significant. Beedell, to take one of them, is found in the Tiverton district of Devon, and also in Somerset. It probably means beadle there, and we need not worry unduly when it appears with 'ea' or 'i' instead of 'ee'. Vowels, as we have seen, are freely interchangeable in dialects—John Read in Blackmore's *Lorna Doone* is Jan Ridd. But when we get Buddle or Buddles, which in the Mendips we related to lead-smelting, we need to consider whether it may not be derived from *bódl*, 'dwelling house', and in Devonshire it could equally well spring from one of the Budleighs: Budleigh in Moreton-hampstead or Budleigh Salterton, just as in Hampshire we might have to consider whether it was connected with one of the Buddles incorporated in place-names in both Fording-bridge and on the Isle of Wight. It is, in fact, a name that we cannot be dogmatic about anywhere. In Staffordshire it could even be a corruption of Biddulph.

Yarde is not the only surname in the West that reflects peculiarities of land-tenure. The best known of these is Buckland, which in other parts of England could be related to the male deer, or to the beech tree. In Devonshire, where it is such a common element in place-names, it usually means book- or charter-land. Faulkland, by contrast, means folk-land and suggests land held by free tenants. By the same token Francombe and Frankham must mean 'freeman'. Under the Forest Laws there were Free Suitors and Suitors at Large. The Free Suitors enjoyed certain privileges in return for such duties as driving the Forest for ponies, cattle, and sheep. They also served on the jury at the Coroner's inquest on any corpse found in the Forest. The Suitors at Large were landowners and tenants who enjoyed rights of commonage. So there can be considerable significance in such names.

In contrast to those of East Anglia, Devonshire surnames derived from places are not overwhelmingly those of towns or villages, but of local topographical features which would be known to everyone living in the community in which

59

they arose. Most of them are notably earthy: Clampytte (Claypit), Fosse (ditch), Furzen (furze), Gribble (crab tree), Haye (hedge or enclosure), Knappe (hill summit), Heird (sheep farm), Kurne (*cweorn*, mill), Twitchen (crossways or place where a road forks). This is a common name in Devonshire, with such variants as Tichner. Several of those just named have dialect modifications. Fosse may be Forse, Vos, or Vose in the Doulting or Shepton Mallet districts of Somerset, which bestrides the Fosse Way. As this trackway passes either through or along the boundaries of other counties it gives rise to surnames in Wiltshire, Warwickshire and even Nottinghamshire; but an incorporated 'v' is peculiar to the South West.

As there are many place-names in Devonshire derived from *bearu*, 'grove', which include the many Beers, surnames incorporating the element are common, although the De la Beres originate in Surrey, and the name is not infrequent elsewhere. The Aclands derive their name from a grove of oaks near Acland Barton in Landkey. Bowdon, 'curved hill', of which Bowden may be a corruption in the West, is not confined to Devon; but as there are at least seventeen places in the county bearing the name there is a strong presumption that it arises there if no evidence can be produced of a different origin. Bawden, however, is probably a local form of Baldwin. Cole and Coleman are names that cannot be linked to any specific county; but Coleridge, the name borne by the poet and a former Lord Chief Justice, is definitely a Devonshire name. On linguistic grounds, an even stronger claim could be made for the name of the present Lord Chief Justice, Lord Widgery, a typically Devonshire name in which 'ery' could well be a corruption of 'worthy', as Badgery is of Badgeworthy, Pinkery of Pinkworthy, and Brightery of Brightworthy.

There is a West Country rhyme:

> *Crocker, Cruwys and Copplestone*
> *When the Conqueror came were at home.*

Since not one of these suggests an origin peculiar to the county it is difficult to see why they were singled out in this way. Crocker means potter in the West as it does everywhere else. But what is the source of Crober, found near it in local directories? It seems to be a name closely associated with the Tavistock district. Can it be from 'crib', and be the name given to a man who made mangers for fodder? And what of Cobbledick? Was the original bearer of the name a 'Dick' who prepared the cob for the stout walls of the cottages we find in the lovely villages below Exmoor? Tupper, we know, was the name given to the man who rammed mud strengthened with straw to produce it. No countryman needs to have the association of 'Tup' with 'Ram' explained to him.

Despite the pride in pre-Conquest families expressed in the couplet just quoted, Devonshire was one of the three English counties most favoured by men from across the Channel. Courtenay, chief of these names, is said to be derived from an old French epic and to mean *court nez*, the name given to an ancestor who had his nose cut off by a Saracen. Pomeroy, another French name renowned in Devon, means 'apple orchard'. Radulphus de la Pomeroy, who came from a place of that name in Normandy, held sixty manors at Domesday, fifty-eight of them in the county, with a castle at Berry Pomeroy. The family fell from eminence during the reign of Edward VI when Sir Thomas Pomeroy resisted the Reformation and lost his estates to the Seymours. The de Rudevilles modified their name to Ruddle. Defoe has an account of the laying of a ghost in 1720 by the Rev. Samuel Ruddle, vicar of Launceston. When Baring-Gould was at Lew Trenchard, one of Parson Ruddle's descendants was a gamekeeper. In fact, Baring-Gould has several instances of descendants of Conquest favourites fallen on evil days. He mentions a carrier between Lew Down and Tavistock who at this death was buried without a gravestone at Lew Trenchard, yet bore a distinguished Norman name. The last members of the de Valence family, which at one time held the earldom of Pembroke, lingered on as tenant farmers of land their ancestors had owned. There is, of course, no end to such family histories, and no reason why families should not suffer such ebb and flow. Others fared better by adapting themselves to new conditions, as did the Tremletts, whose name is from *Les Trois Minettes*. They became prosperous clothiers at Tiverton, the town to which John Heathcote, a lace manufacturer, came from Leicestershire when the Luddites smashed his machines. Among French names that have continued are Angwin (from Anjou), Burgin and Burgoyne (from Burgundy), Brittain (from Brittany) and Champernown (from Champayne).

It is impossible to run one's finger down a column of surnames in a West Country Telephone Directory without stopping short at a score that pose questions. There are the Hockeys, Hockins, Hockings, Hockridges and so on that suggest hawking, and when we reach the 'L's we get the Lillicraps, in which 'crap' suggests croft, or enclosure, the Loveridges and the Luscombes. The 'M's bring the Metherells, Muggeridges, and Mudges; the 'N's the Nankivells, which means 'the valley of the horse', and the Nosworthys. Happily the 'P's bring us back to familiar ground with 'Pether' in such names as Petheridge and Petherick, which we recognise as the West Country form of Peter. Shopland and Shapland raise again the question of one vowel being substituted for another. Shap in Devon must mean sheep. This kind of change is easy enough to understand, except in terminals, which introduce many traps for the unwary. Whereas a final -am in the East might be from a place-name ending in -ham, in the West it is probably from -combe. Similarly, many -yl and -el endings are from hill. No doubt the ancestor of our old friend Uncle Tom Cobley in the Widdecombe Fair song was a man named Cobleigh.

These are instances of shortened names; but in the West of England it is more characteristic to lengthen them by intruding a vowel between two consonants to produce names like Faraway, Westaway, Greenaway, and so on. A curious one is Hannaford, which may be from the Old English *hān*, 'stone or rock', to indicate a ford with a stone base. Baring-Gould explained this by writing: 'In the West of England the ear cannot endure a harsh conjunction of consonants'; but he might have extended this to explain the way his countrymen played fast and loose with consonants as well as vowels. One habit was the adding of a consonant at the end of a name, noted a moment ago in connection with Dayman. We find it also in Simond or Simmond for Simon, and Hammond for Hamon. Even commoner is the addition of 'g' as we have it in Perking for Perkin. And even more puzzling than these is the substitution in the middle of a name, not of a vowel but a consonant. A place called Cutliffton on the edge of Dartmoor became Cudlipton, and gave us the surname Cudlip. Clobbury is probably from Cliffbury, Lipton from Cliffton, and Lippincott from Luffincott. But there is one fact to be noted in connection with these vernacular corruptions. Even the substitutions of 'V' for 'F' and 'Z' for 'S' in surnames do not appear in the early Rolls, which were compiled by clerks trained by monks from the Continent who did not countenance such dialectical indulgences, and the conclusion to be drawn from this is that such names came in when oral custom rather than record determined the form of names, which means, of course, that they were late.

Although it is the rural character of Devonshire that has determined its main surname structure, there must be many craft names that could only have arisen in the towns. One that we should like to know more about is Pewterer. There was a Thomas Pewterer working in Barnstaple in 1343; but even then the trade was ancient. We know that pewter making was practised in several West Country towns from the Roman occupation until the beginning of the nineteenth century. The many pewter vessels in West Country churches shows how flourishing the industry must have been during the period in which the common people were acquiring surnames.

Finally, we must not forget the Sea Dogs. 'Drake he was a Devon man, and ruled the Devon seas'. But was he? According to Sir Thomas Smith, Elizabeth I's Secretary of State, writing in *De Republica Anglorum*, he was the son of an Isle of Wight fisherman and took the name of Drake by choice, not inheritance. There is also an ongoing argument

63

as to whether the line of Grenvilles that produced Sir Richard of the *Revenge* was the same as the one that sprang from Grainville, though I don't know where else it could have come from. Fortunately, there appears to be no difference of opinion about the Gilbert family, with six hundred years of history behind the name in Devonshire, producing the Sir Humphrey who played so great a part in the early colonisation of America.

Of Cornwall it is sometimes said that there are more saints in the county than there are in Heaven, despite the number of sinners that John Wesley was able to bring to contrition in the eighteenth century. In view of the number of place-names that incorporate the names of Celtic saints it is not surprising that Richard Blewett, who made a study of Cornish surnames in 1953, should have found that one-seventh of them were derived from saints or apostles, or had a religious connection of one kind or another. Among the more interesting of his finds, apart from this, was that 'gear' in Angear, Tregear, and other place-name surnames is cognate with car, 'a fort or camp'. In St. Ives this becomes Care, after passing through such forms as Kear, Keyr, and Gaire.

As everyone knows, the starting point for a study of Cornish surnames is the couplet,

> *By Tre, Ros, Car, Lan, Pol, and Pen*
> *You well may know all Cornish men.*

But we soon discover that the list is by no means comprehensive. The first of the county's historians, William Borlase, who as vicar of St. Just for forty years could always count on having a congregation of a thousand to listen to his sermons, had a true Cornish name which began with 'Bor' and meant 'the green summit'. Like those listed in the couplet it was a toponymic. 'Tre' denotes farmstead or village, 'Ros' a heath or moor, 'Lan' a church, 'Pol' a pool, 'Pen' a headland; but many names need to be taken back to their first appearance before we can recognise the meaning of the surnames that have emerged from them. Thus Boscastle was Boterelescastel when it was held at the beginning of the fourteenth century by William de Botereus, a name that indicates an origin in Normandy. This was Anglicised into Botterell or Botterill, which without the prefix 'de' could be from a nickname (*boterel*, 'toad'), or from buttery.

But even the prefix can be deceptive. Knyvett is said to be derived from a former name of Launceston. The story goes that Othomarius, lord of Launceston, was deprived of his possessions for taking up arms against the Conqueror; but that these were restored to him when he married a Norman lady, and the name de Knyvett was taken by his descendants. This is an incredible name since no such place has been found to exist on the Continent. In this case, the probable explanation is that at some stage 'de' was a misreading of 'le'. This would make sense since the word *knyvet* is thought to have been a French form of 'knight'.

Bullivant is another Cornish name with more than one possible derivation. It may be from *pol y font*, 'the head of the spring', or from *bon enfant*, 'good child'. Bonallack would then be a kindred name, from *bon aller*, 'God speed'. So, generally speaking, the couplet is the safest if not the most inclusive guide, and most of the names beginning with 'Tre' are authenticated in the villages of their origin. The Treddinicks have their memorials where they started, and a whole host of kindred names spring to mind, including Trefusis, Tregelles, Treloar, Tremaine, and Tremelling, which is another surname adding a final 'g' to the place-name, in this case Tremellen. Among the most famous Trevillicks was the William of St. Mary's, who started the marketing of spring flowers in London.

The 'Lans' are not quite so safe. The nineteenth-century explorers, John and Richard Lander of Higher Pengelly, derived their name from an occupation. A lander was a man stationed at the mouth of a mine-shaft to receive the bucket—literally to land it. The Lanyons take their name from a place, but not a Cornish church town. The family came to England with Isabella, wife of Edward II, from Lannion in Brittany and settled in Cornwall. And, incidentally, a Cornish name ending in -er, which is usually accepted as an occupation name, Hurler, is the name originally given to a man who was expert in hurling the ball in a game peculiar to Cornwall, which is described in Carew's *Survey of Cornwall.*

'Bos', an alternative to 'Trev' in meaning a dwelling, has produced many surnames, including Boscawen, which reached eminence in Hugh, Recorder of Truro, who died in 1641, and whose grandson, the first Viscount Falmouth, was ennobled after representing three Cornish constituencies in Parliament and serving as Steward of the Duchy of Lancaster and Lord Warden of the Stannaries.

There remain many Cornish forms of common name-elements that continue to defy definition. In Yorkshire 'hale' usually means rock, from the Old Norse *hallr*. In Cornwall it has several topographical possibilities. It may mean moor. As early as 1327 there was a Stephano del Hal, who is presumed to have been Stephen of the Moor. But it could be from the Old English *halh* and mean nook, or even from *hālig*, and mean holy.

It would take a much better scholar than I am to give the meanings of even the commonest Cornish names that do not fall into the broadest categories. As a Forest Verderer the Cornish surname, Jewel, fascinates me and perhaps tempts me out of my depth. The yew happens to be the only tree, so far as I know, that has kept its Celtic name, Iw. So although the yew is rare in the far West now, I am tempted to derive the surname from it. The tree is only found in large numbers in Surrey, Kent, the Cotswolds, and the North West of England today; but as a symbol of eternity associated with churchyards it must surely have been common formerly in a county as religious as Cornwall. It has, however, been suggested that the second element in Jewel is *haël*, 'generous', and the first *Jud*, 'lord or chief'. If this is correct the name would be of Breton origin and mean 'generous lord'. Another apparently simple element, 'hare', which is a Cornish surname, might be thought to refer to the animal; but in Cornish *hyr* means long, so the name was given to a tall man. As there is a Cornish surname Enhare, 'the long', this seems the more probable.

Then there is that commonest of all surnames, Smith,

which in Cornwall becomes Angove, from *Gof* and *Gov*, which are Celtic words for blacksmith, and turn up in Warwickshire and Worcestershire from the fourteenth century onwards as the surnames Goff and Goffe. In Devonshire the same name is found as Gove. So perhaps it should not take a Cornishman to recognise in Angove, 'the blacksmith'. But could anyone but a Cornishman recognise Tyak as the name for a farmer or husbandman? So Cornish surnames are not for the amateur; but when we have put our dictionaries and gazetteers away, we may still reflect with gratitude on three authentic Cornish names, Keats, Opie, and Couch, and on such experiences as hearing a choir of true-hearted Cornishmen sing 'And shall Trelawny die?'

CHAPTER FOUR
The West Midlands

In travelling from the extreme east to the extreme west of Southern England we found in every county surnames that reflected the mixed origins of even our longest established families. French influences were strong everywhere. When we move northward into the West Midlands we find Celtic influences increasing, with such typically Welsh surnames as Gough, Gwynne, and Lloyd—which had been Floyd in Devonshire and Cornwall—recorded in Herefordshire and Shropshire two hundred years before the Welsh in Wales so much as thought of adopting surnames. Some of them would be nicknames given to Welshmen who had crossed the Marches into England, most of which survive in corrupted forms. Maddocks is one Welsh name that confused the English so much that it is found in at least twelve different spellings. As Madock it is a Domesday name in Gloucestershire; as Madoc it has been in Shropshire since the thirteenth century. All are from the Welsh Madog, 'godly'. Meredith is held by Reaney to be the source of Beddoe and Beddoes; but it may be thought more likely that they are derived from Ap-Eddoes, 'son of Eddoe', which is still a Shropshire name, just as Bennion is Ap-Ennion, a Welsh personal name derived from *enyon*, 'anvil', with Benyon and Binyon as variants. Powell, which as a surname came later, has an equally ancient root. Like Howell it is from Howel, king of the West Welsh before the Conquest, although it may have come to some parts of England from Brittany.

As nicknames are early everywhere, origins are often uncertain. Corbet, which means raven, was a nickname given to a man with black hair. It is thought to have started with a Roger Corbet, or le Corbet, who came to England with the Conqueror; but as it is incorporated in several place-names it would be absurd to argue that all the present-day Corbets had a common ancestor. Gittings and Gittins, which have a similar meaning, are derived from the Welsh *gethin*, 'dusky or swarthy'. Povey, a Gloucestershire word for owl, is one of several nicknames given to men who had the reputation of being 'night birds'. I don't know whether the initial 'P' in this name is significant or not; but Welsh influences were so all-pervading in Shropshire in times of early settlement that the surname Sayce was introduced from the Welsh *sais*, 'Saxon', to identify a solitary Englishman living there.

The most persistent Continental influences in the West Midlands came into Gloucestershire when Edward III brought Flemish weavers over to teach the English their craft, and settled many of them in the Cotswolds. Others followed to build up a colony that flourished through the centuries and was greatly strengthened after the revocation of the Edict of Nantes in 1685 by Huguenot Protestants. Memorials to these clothier families are to be seen in the many Cotswold churches they either rebuilt or enlarged. Chipping Campden, Fairford, and Northleach are examples. William Grevel's name will never be forgotten; but he was only one of many local benefactors. The Clutterbucks, who came from the Low Countries, were prominent in Gloucestershire life for many generations. One was mayor of Gloucester in 1545, another in 1646, and a Stephen Clutterbuck was mayor of Bristol in 1739. Other prominent names among clothier benefactors were Fortey, Holbrow, Malpass, Prout, Pettitt, Tame, and Phillimore.

The Huguenot clothier families concentrated themselves in the villages that have Stroud as their capital, attracted by the plentiful supply of soft water that ran into the streams from the Midford sands overlying the Upper Lias clay. So prosperous did they become that at the height of its fame Stroud alone required more than two million fleeces a year to keep its mills going. Among the most prominent of the

Huguenots were the Sheppards of Stroud and Minchin-hampton, the Playnes of Longford, the Packers of Painswick, the Peglars of Uley, the Phelps, the Dallaways, and the Wattses, supported in their mills by those who bore occu-pation names already noted in Somerset: Tozers, Tuckers, Webbs and Webbers, some of whom rose to be master clothiers. Thomas Fuller, who himself bore an occupation name, referred in the *Worthies* to 'a prime Dutch cloth maker in Gloucestershire named Web', and a Tucker became Dean of Gloucester. But despite the many Webbs, the number of weavers called Weaver increases notably in Gloucestershire and Worcestershire.

So widespread was the industry that in 1712 Sir Robert Atkyns, the county historian whose family, incidentally, produced four judges, wrote: 'The clothing trade is so eminent in this county that no other manufacture deserves a mention'. Consequently, when Yorkshire took over as the centre of the woollen industry, a certain James Tait visited Gloucester to study the machinery in its mills. But this was the beginning of the end for the Cotswold clothiers. When Edward Sheppard, who had been its leading figure, failed in 1835, the bell tolled. Members of the Fluck, Gazard, Apperley, Cumley, and Darrot families tried to keep the trade alive; but they could not be expected to succeed where as shrewd a man as Edward Sheppard, or Shepphard, as the name is sometimes spelt, had failed. But many of the Flemish and Huguenot family names survive. Hiatt, Hyett, Hyatt are all forms of the name of one of these clothier families of Minchinhampton.

As early as 1614 a group of Huguenot glass makers moved into the Forest of Dean, attracted by the supply of timber available for their furnaces. They also introduced names that have persisted in the county. In 1880 a guide to the Forest of Dean was published by John Bellows, whose first recorded ancestor must clearly have been either a maker of bellows or a bellows-blower.

As the surname Whittington is from a place-name in at least eight northern and midland counties, it can hardly be claimed for Gloucestershire; but the redoubtable 'Dick',

Lord Mayor of London, can certainly be claimed. He was a Stroud clothier and benefactor. Contrary to the fairy tale version of his story, he was born of a knightly family seated at Pauntley Court before removing to Notgrove in the middle of the sixteenth century.

The great manorial names of Gloucestershire are well known, headed as they are by the Berkeleys of Berkeley Castle, the most remarkable case in the whole of England of the survival of the old nobility. There are place-name complications for some of the families claiming descent. The banking family of Barclay, for example, who do not claim descent from the family, probably derive their name from the place, although they reached East Anglia and London from Scotland. On the other hand, a family that definitely descends from the Berkeleys of Berkeley Castle does not bear the name. It is that of Kingscote of Kingscote, the first of whom had a confirmation of the manor from his uncle, Maurice de Berkeley, in 1188 and the family have been at Kingscote ever since.

When we turn to the families who created so much of the West Midlands scene as we have it today, the fruit farmers, we are especially fortunate in that Ralph Bigland, Garter King of Arms from 1780 to 1784, had churchyard inscriptions copied for nearly all the parishes in Gloucestershire. One of the most stalwart of the yeoman families of both Gloucestershire and Herefordshire are the Holders of Taynton, a name that appears in the Hundred Roll of 1274. Professor Finberg, in *Gloucestershire Studies*, discusses the progress of this typical West Midlands family through the centuries in a way that gives the reader the true feel of the local way of life. In 1538 a John Holder of Churcham bequeathed to one of his sons a 'house to lay his fruit in', and to his daughter 'a rudge of ground with fruit trees'. One hundred years later a succeeding John was able to bequeath to his second son, Robert, his best brass kettle and his cider mill in Taynton. From this Robert descended a line of Holders who built the fine farm buildings at Taynton, one of whom left a fascinating MS. diary. This was the Holder who made his cider mill so prosperous that Rudder, another eminent Gloucestershire historian, was able to write:

'This parish is famous for producing a very rich and pleasant cyder'. The Diarist's descendants continued at Taynton House until 1952.

Taynton is near the Herefordshire border, and Herefordshire is another county in which we look for the initial 'P' in surnames as a corruption of 'Ap' for 'son of'. We find it in Pendry, 'son of Henry', and Price, which is Ap-Rhys, the family that produced Sir Uvedale Price (1747-1829), the greatest exponent of the English Picturesque. Another virtuoso associated with Herefordshire was the Richard Payne Knight who built Downton Castle. As heir to the wealth of the Knights who were the great ironmasters of Bridgnorth, Shropshire, he represents the families drawn into the West Midlands—not from Wales or the Continent, but from the industrial region to the east. Another branch of this remarkable family was responsible for the bringing into cultivation of large tracts of Exmoor.

Of these West Midlands counties, Herefordshire long remained the most feudal in character. The Normans adopted its river system for defence against the Welsh, and built the castles that are now in ruins; but which add romance to the county's scenery and attracted the many virtuosos who settled near them in the eighteenth century. Few descendants of the 'lords marcher' remain in occupation of vast estates; but there are many old families with historically evocative names in both Herefordshire and Worcestershire. They include the Mynors of Treago, the Mortimers, whose stronghold was at Wigmore, the Blounts, the Crofts of Croft Castle between Leominster and Ludlow, where they lived from Norman times to 1750, and resumed residence after a break of one hundred and seventy years in 1923, only to convey the estate to the National Trust in a 1957 settlement.

If Worcestershire's local history enthusiasts were asked to say which of the county's surnames was to them most uniquely representative, someone would be sure to suggest Amphlett, a name almost completely confined to the county, which apparently originated at Amflete in Normandy and may still be seen on shop-signs. The same question would be less easily answered in Herefordshire, which has many localised names, some of which are less common now than they were formerly. Blanchflower, for example, a remarkable instance of a long surname that continued in uncorrupted form for seven hundred years in the county, is now rare. But someone in Hereford would be sure to put forward Scudamore as the one distinctively local name, and a good case could certainly be made for it, although it occurs as a place-name at Upton Scudamore, Wiltshire, which was given to Godfrey Escudamore in the middle of the twelfth century; but the Scudamores of Kentchurch Court and Pontrilas Court are equally ancient. They are descended from Walter de Scudamore, who in 1149 gave land to the Abbey of Dore. A fourteenth-century Sir John of Kentchurch, Constable of Goodrich Castle, married a daughter of the great Owen Glendower, and the 'warlike deeds' of Sir James Scudamore are celebrated in Spenser's *Faerie Queene*. The Sir John who was created 1st Viscount Scudamore was a Royalist who devoted his last years to relieving distress among the deprived clergy and restoring the beautiful church at Abbey Dore, which had come into the possession of his family. For this splendid work he engaged the king's carpenter, John Abel, with results for which posterity must continue to bless his name. At Holme Lacy on the Wye are monuments to the branch of the family seated at Holme Lacy House, in which Alexander Pope is said to have written the eulogy to John Kyrle, 'the Man of Ross'. Corruptions of the name are found in Somerset, Warwickshire, and Worcestershire; but its real home is Herefordshire.

Kyrle as a surname first appeared as 'Crul' in 1295. The Kyrle line of baronets, the first of whom married a Scudamore, originated in Much Marcle, near Ross-on-Wye. At first sight, the Herefordshire name of Skyrme might be thought related; but it is much more probable that it is derived from the Old French *eskirmir*, 'fencing master'. Alternatively, it could be Scandinavian.

Several of the leading Herefordshire families have their roots in other counties. The Biddulphs, who have fine monuments at Ledbury, came from Staffordshire. The Vaughans of Kinnersley, seated so long at Bredwardine Castle, came from Shropshire. Their name, which is sometimes spelt Walne, stimulates speculations on the substitution of 'W' for 'V', which are further complicated by the appearance at Much Marcle of the Walwyn family, whose name is romantically associated with the Arthurian romances in which Gwalchgwyn is a white falcon. In parts of France the Anglo-Norman Walwain became Gawain, and this substitution of 'G' for 'W' is said to explain how the name became Gawayne, the son of King Arthur's sister in the romances.

The Harleys, who were settled at Brampton Brian in the fourteenth century, are another Shropshire family in the main line, although the name occurs in Yorkshire. The West Midlands family gave their name to Harley Street, London, and held the Oxford earldom for two generations. Two other Herefordshire surnames, Dansie and Tyrell, illustrate how much easier it is to be dogmatic about places than about persons. Dansie probably means 'Dane's island'; but it could be from Dauntsey, in which the first syllable is a personal name that originated in Wiltshire. In Tyrell we again have a name spelt in a variety of ways. The Tirrels of Hereford have their home at Brinsop Court, north-west of the City; but Walter Tirrel is a name in the Essex Domesday, and has been in Gloucestershire records since the twelfth century and Worcestershire records since the thirteenth. The one thing that can be said with conviction about it is that it is French in origin and was a nickname given to a man who 'pulled on the reins', or as we should say, was given to taking 'the bit between his teeth'.

But of all these family names the one that takes the prize for variety of spellings and peripatetic energy is Baskerville, which must be derived from Boscherville in Normandy. It appears first in Gloucestershire records in 1127, occurs in Shropshire in the thirteenth century, and makes its way round the Midlands ringing the changes through Baskerfield, Basketfield, Baskeyfield, Baskwell, Pesterfield and Pusterfield. As the Herefordshire branch of the family can trace their

75

pedigree back to the time of Edward I it may very well have started with a Conquest family of that name.

It may be said that these Midland families would inevitably circulate freely, and the variety in their spellings needs no further explanation; but the many ways in which a name as common as Allcott, 'old cottage', is spelt can only be evidence of illiteracy, and suggest that they post-dated the recording of names by French clerks. The intruded vowel, so common a dialect feature in the West of England, is found in the Midlands in Hathaway, from Heathway, which occurs in Gloucestershire and Herefordshire as well as in Warwickshire as the name of Shakespeare's wife. Another widely distributed West Midlands name is Barrett. It has been in Worcestershire since 1185, and could be a name given in these heavily wooded counties either to a man who made wooden barrels or as a nickname to a man who looked like one. But alternatively it could be from the Old French *barrette*, a cap or bonnet, which would make it an occupation name for a maker of headwear. Hatterall or Hatterel, found in the Midlands, has the same meaning. The word 'haterel' is used in the fifteenth-century York Plays for dress or attire. Cadwal, in Gloucestershire is found as Caddell or Cadle, and in Herefordshire as Caldwall. Caswall, or Caswell, is a Leominster name, which was borne by Sir George Caswall, whose family were impoverished when the South Sea Bubble burst. The surname occurs in seventeen different forms derived from place-names in eight counties. In Herefordshire it is from Crasswall, in Worcestershire from Kerswell, and means 'water-cress stream'.

Another woodland name is Hakluyt, which means 'hack little', so was a nickname given to a lazy woodcutter. It has been a surname along the Welsh border since the fourteenth century. Locally, the most distinguished Hakluyts were the Heaton Hall family, members of which represented Leominster in Parliament for two hundred years; nationally, the most distinguished Hakluyt was the Richard who chronicled the early voyages of the English navigators. Occupation names reflecting the woodland character of the West Midlands increase as we travel through Worcestershire into Warwickshire, where Woodward is a typical local name. Acton, from 'oak-ton', is another. It occurs early in Warwickshire; but the principal families bearing it are the Actons of Ombersley in Worcestershire, and the Shropshire Actons, the Roman Catholic family that produced Lord Acton, the historian. As in the West Midlands the usual meaning of stock is stump, Stocker is an occupation name for the woodman who grubbed up the stumps of felled trees—the man who in Kent and Sussex would be called Stubber. And Tolley, an Evesham name which first appeared as Tolle in the 1327 Worcestershire Subsidy Roll, could be from the dialect word 'toll', used thereabouts for a clump of trees.

Worcestershire was largely by-passed by the Romans once they had established defences along the Severn. The reason for this is that the county's approach from Gloucestershire was constantly under threat from tribesmen on the Malvern Hills, while to the east and north stretched vast areas of forest, which meant that there was little for the Romans to go for in the county except the salt at Droitwich. So the Hwicce continued to occupy an area extending to Wychwood in Oxfordshire, under the rule of an under-king who reigned from Worcester. In A.D. 679 the bishop of the tribe made that city the head of a powerful See, so dominant that the life-style of the county became ecclesiastical rather than martial, and in consequence historians have had the immeasurable advantage of access to local records, carefully kept by monks and their clerks. These records, as we should expect, show a mingling of the foreign names of immigrant workmen with such pre-Conquest names as Elgar, which has been a recorded Worcestershire name since the thirteenth century, and belongs to the England of Hereward and Baldwin. Among the new names was Mence, with such variants as Maunce, Mayers, and Mense, which the Mayers of Ombersely trace back to Mentz on the Rhine.

The number of different names found in the records suggests that they are a subject for local rather than general survey; but to anyone who knows Worcestershire even cursorily many of them are evocative and conjure up pictures of country life, if only because they are familiar on personal shop-signs—now, so rapidly disappearing—and on inn signs like the Lygon Arms at Broadway, and the Foley Arms and Hornyold Arms at Malvern, reminding us of the family seated at Hanley Castle. Recent take-overs of small local breweries have meant that there are now fewer names of old brewing families on village inn signs than there used to be, and fewer old-established licensee families like the one that kept the 'Fleece' at Bretforton, near Evesham, which remained in one family for five hundred years, and is remembered by visitors as the place where the cracks between the stone flags were whitened to prevent access to witches.

In these hop-growing counties, in which 'The Hop Pole' is still a familiar sign, we should expect to hear tales of mighty drinkers, and they are not lacking, although gone are the days described in *Poor Robin's Almanack*, when

> *You may make pretty tipple if so you've a mind't*
> *With hops and with malt for a penny a pint.*

The word 'tipler' has changed its meaning since those lines were written. Today it means a man who indulges to excess in liquor. In the time of the first Elizabeth it simply meant a man who had a licence to sell it. A document is preserved in the Corporation Archives at Warwick listing 'Such Typlers and alehouse-keepers as the Justices of the Peax have returned to me this Michilmas Session. Thies underwritten were returnyd by Sir Thomas Lucy and Humphrey Peto, Equire'. To obtain such a licence a tipler would enter into a recognisance for the good governance of his house and for abstaining from the use of unlawful games 'during the time of his tiplinge'. So when we meet the surname Tipler we may recognise it as originally that of a tapster or seller of ale. Consequently Tapster and Tapper are good West Midlands names for men whose ancestors were inn-keepers, or ale-tappers, with Tapster as the feminine form of the name, just as Baxter is of Baker, and Webster of Webber. Taphouse, however, now a well-known Oxford name, is from a place-name in Cornwall.

Despite these entirely reputable origins, the licence to confer respectability on all names beginning with 'Tip' or 'Tap' is subject to severe restriction. The first Tiplady could only have been a man who had a reputation for taking liberties with ladies. What these liberties were it would be imprudent to speculate upon, since in its alternative spelling of Toplady it was the name of the author of the hymn 'Rock of Ages'. The Tippers, however, are entirely respectable in origin. They were men who made arrow-heads or 'tips', and the Tippells, Tipples, and Tippins were merely descendants of a gentleman named Theobald, who was thought entitled to a more affectionate form of address.

If these appear to be frivolous speculations, it must be allowed that Drinkwater is an authentic and no less appropriate name in the West Midlands. The Georgian poet, John Drinkwater, confessed pleasure in reflecting that:

> *from my sires*
> *I draw the blood of England's midmost shires.*

The name makes its first appearance in the thirteenth century in Shropshire. It also appears early in Gloucestershire; but it is unlikely that it can have been a source of pride in days when ale was the drink of all but the poorest, and certainly far safer than water except on the Malvern Hills. It was proof of the extreme poverty of the Franciscans when they first settled in England that it was written of them: 'I have seen the brothers drink ale so sour that some would have preferred to drink water'.

Three famous names that regard the West Midlands as their home are Throckmorton, Lyttelton, and Kinnersley. Throckmorton means a mere with a bridge or wharf supported by trestles (from throck). Lyttelton has been a Worcestershire surname since 1358 and has a long association with Hagley Hall, built by the 1st Lord Lyttelton, but it occurs as a place-name in at least eight counties in one form or another. Kinnersley is derived from place-names in Herefordshire, Worcestershire, and Shropshire. Cyne, as an element in similar names means 'royal', or 'king's'; but Kinnersley first appears as de Kinardesle, suggesting a

79

place-name origin that is closest to Kennerleigh in Devon, *Cyneweard's leah*, which incorporates a personal name related to Kenilworth (Warwickshire) and Kenderchurch (Herefordshire). In these a woman's name Cynehild, is incorporated in Kenilworth, while Kenderchurch means St. Cynidr's church.

Pardoe, a West Midlands name since the fourteenth century, is an oath name which must have originated in *de par Dieu*, 'in God's name', or *pour Dieu*, reminding us of Chaucer's line: 'I have a wyfe, pardee, as well as thow'. There was a Christian Pardoe living in Worcester in 1794, aged 103, and the name is found in Norfolk as Purdy.

These names bring home to us the value of such writers as Langland and Chaucer in providing clues to vernacular uses of old phrases in surnames. Wagstaffe, a jocular name for a beadle, would be introduced in this way. Perhaps the most useful source-book for such names is Wycliffe's translation of the Bible (1382), where words that survive only in dialect appear on almost every page. These dialect variations are especially important when we try to identify local peculiarities in common personal names. The West Midlands have a particularly apt example of this. Whereas in Wales a final 's' was added to a personal name to produce such surnames as Jones, Roberts, Williams and so on, in Worcestershire and Warwickshire 'en' was added to a personal name to produce Jacken, Nicken, Tommen, Kytten, Watten, Gibben, Hicken, Hitchen, and many others. A local character named Pullen played a harmonium at St. Anne's Well, Malvern, for fifty years until his death in 1936. Dr. Reaney found forty names of this type not recorded elsewhere in the Subsidy Rolls for Worcestershire (1327) and Warwickshire (1332). Griffen and Griffin appear in these records as pet forms of the Welsh Gruffudd.

A surname common to many counties, Mitton or Mytton, which means 'meeting of streams', found a home in Shropshire in a family that intermarried with neighbouring long-established families to such an extent that they all became cousins sooner or later. They first became wealthy through the marriage of Sir Thomas Mytton of Halston, Shropshire, with Eleanor, daughter of John de Burgh, who brought vast estates and the royal Cambrian blood of Powys into the family. Later alliances were with the Delves of Doddington, Greys of Enville, Grevilles of Milcote, Corbets of Stoke, Owens of Condover, and Myddeltons of Chirk. After five hundred years the family inheritance was dissipated by the eccentric John Mytton (1796-1834), squire of Halston. The Kynastons are another Shropshire family claiming descent from the princes of Powys.

In contrast to the Myttons, we have the old Roman Catholic family of Benthall, who in the sixteenth century built the fine hall that bears their name. After continuing as a small but moderately prosperous landed family in Shropshire for several generations the male line died out in 1720, and the property passed away from them. As with the Crofts, a Benthall descendant returned to repurchase the old family home and pass it on after a few years to the National Trust. Meanwhile a branch of the family established itself in Essex on a farm that acquired the family name during the seventeenth century. The Essex Benthalls eventually founded a prosperous business in Maldon, and it was a member of the Maldon branch, Frank Benthall, who founded the store at Kingston in Surrey. Another enterprising West Midlands family, the Earlys, went into industry nearer home, and expanded at Witney the blanket-making business founded by the Wenhams in the fifteenth century, and so restored in Oxfordshire something of the prosperity that centuries earlier had brought wealth to the Gloucestershire Cotswolds. Thomas Early founded his business in 1660.

As we move into Warwickshire we immediately think of ourselves as being in Shakespeare country, and rejoice to find Shakespearean names on every hand. The Lucys were lords of Charlecote, four miles east of Stratford-upon-Avon, from the thirteenth century until 1945, when Sir Montgomerie Fairfax-Lucy conveyed the estate to the National Trust. The first Sir Thomas Lucy of Charlecote was Shakespeare's Justice Shallow. At Compton Wynyates, one of the county's architectural jewels, we are reminded of John Talbot, 1st Earl of Shrewsbury, another name that occurs in several counties, upon which cynics might comment that this is not surprising since its most likely derivation is from the Old French *talebot*, 'bandit'.

Although Compton is a name found in other counties, it has special significance in Warwickshire because a surprising number of compound place-names incorporate it. Another West Midlands family, the Verneys, are now chiefly associated with Buckinghamshire; but the name is probably derived from the family at Compton Verney in Warwickshire, to which it came from France. Among the memorials to the Verneys in the church at Compton Verney is one to John Verney, Master of the Rolls. Another Warwickshire place-name that may have produced a good old Warwickshire surname is Chivers, which may be a nickname from the Anglo-French *chivere*, but more probably is a corruption of the place-name Chilvers.

At Baginton, Warwickshire, are the ruins of the castle built by Sir William Bagot, who figures in Shakespeare's *Richard II*. There is a brass to his memory in the church. But of all the names that are associated with Shakespearean characters in Warwickshire, and provide as firm a clue to Shakespeare's own character as the family names of Dorset do to Hardy's, the one that counts above all others is Arden, his mother's name. The blood of the Ardens was in Shakespeare's veins and powered the speeches of Henry V at Agincourt. According to Horace Round, who never erred on the side of charity, the Ardens not only enjoyed clear descent from Aelfwine, Sheriff of Warwickshire under Edward the Confessor, whose son's lands fill more than four columns in Domesday Book, but continued in unbroken possession of those lands 'at least as late as the days of Queen Elizabeth', which is the same thing as saying as late as Shakespeare's time.

CHAPTER FIVE

The Eastern Kingdoms

During the centuries immediately after the Conquest East Anglia was the wealthiest and most populous part of England. Norwich was its capital, and by the close of the thirteenth century had attracted new inhabitants from hundreds of surrounding villages. Some of them would have nicknames on arrival; but few, if any, would have adopted family surnames by which they could be identified in official records. So they were given the names of the villages from which they had come and these eventually became hereditary. Even today there are probably as many as two hundred of these place-names still in use in East Anglia, and many more in other parts of England.

East Anglian surnames were thus an obvious field for detailed study by researchers in the English Surnames Survey mentioned in the Introduction to this book, and students are referred to Richard McKinley's *Norfolk and Suffolk Surnames in the Middle Ages* for a scientific analysis of them. In his Introduction to Richard McKinley's work, Professor Everitt says: 'In early 14th century Norwich, for example, nearly half the freemen had locative surnames derived from other places, and in Lynn the proportion was nearly two-thirds'. As we should expect, the earliest of these names were of villages in the immediate vicinity; but gradually the catchment area expanded until by the middle of the Tudor period it included not only villages at a distance, but chartered boroughs, showing that mobility had developed over the whole of East Anglia, with men carrying their skills from one town to another. These names continued to proliferate as wealth and prosperity increased until the Black Death killed off more than half the population in the middle of the fourteenth century, reducing numbers but not proportions.

Although by the Tudor period it could no longer be assumed that all who bore the same name were of the same family, since the first man who came from Debenham, shall we say, to Ipswich would be given that name to identify him, no matter how many Debenham men had been given the same name when they settled in other East Anglian towns. In fact, of course, they were all closely related through intermarriage among their Debenham ancestors, and it might be argued that the bearing of a village name as a surname is better proof of local ancestry than other names of real or alleged parents. Debenham is a good example for the purpose of such an argument, because it continues in use to a quite remarkable extent both locally and nationally, either in its original form or corrupted into either Deadman of Debnam, just as Tuddenham is corrupted to Tudman. By the same token one of the most prolific and distinguished East Anglian families, the Buxtons, wherever they are found today, are more likely to have derived their name from a village in Norfolk than from Derbyshire.

Once the major migrations had been completed, the communities that remained most settled were those in abbey towns, where there was security under the benevolent rule of a rich foundation. A detailed list of the tenants of lands owned by the abbey of Bury St. Edmunds from soon after the Conquest has survived, and it is of unique interest as the earliest comprehensive list of peasant names. Among other things it shows that not only did the link of a surname with a place of origin remain strong, but that the link of a family with an occupation continued through several generations as a matter of course. This is a feature found all over England up to the end of the eighteenth century, and reminds us how much more meaningful occupation names were formerly than they are today, when a man with six sons might put them into six different occupations.

One name that became common soon after the Conquest, Hayward, is especially interesting because it may be the source of non-patrician branches of the Howard family. In the parish register at Horringer, Suffolk, the occupation 'hayward' is actually spelt Howard. But it is equally interesting because the hayward was the man who guarded the 'haye', or hedged enclosure, and the number of Haywards recorded bears testimony to the richness of the cornlands of East Anglia at an early date, and also to the stimulation of greed which seems to be the inevitable accompaniment of affluence. So the men of East Anglia anticipated the wise advice of *Piers Plowman* to:

> *have an horne and be haywarde,*
> *and liggen oute a nyghtes,*
> *and kepe my corn in my croft*
> *from pykers and theves.*

Not all these 'pykers and theves' were local. During the Middle Ages the wealth of the abbeys was immeasurably increased by the acquisition of sacred relics, which drew countless hosts of pilgrims to such shrines as those of Walsingham and Bury St. Edmunds, and these produced such surnames as Pegrum and Palmer. Some of these monastic estates were owned by older foundations in other counties, which would frequently send skilled craftsmen to train recruits to the crafts introduced to new estates. So we find names cropping up from parts of England which call for explanation and may be socially revealing. The presence of Sussex names in Norfolk would be due in some measure to the fact that Lewes Priory owned land there. There is, perhaps, no great significance in that factor as a rule, since similar reasons for immigration are found in most counties; but when it continues over a long period, or introduces an unusually fertile stock, it may be very significant indeed. The number of Yorkshire names in East Anglia, for example, draws attention to the movement that has continued ever since the Middle Ages down the east of England from North to South. My own view is that this is largely due to the feeling of kinship that always seems to have been felt between families of Scandinavian origin.

But even when questions of this kind have been answered there remains the general question of why East Anglia has such a large number of surnames that have never been common elsewhere. The most probable explanation of this is that Norwich has always been to an exceptional degree a provincial capital, into which the clever boys of Norfolk have gravitated and been retained by the county, whereas the clever boys of Essex, for example, gravitated into London and were lost. Another factor has been that East Anglia was settled by a number of small races that did not colonise outside the region in the way their more numerous rivals did.

One of the joys of going through such lists as that of the tenants of the abbot of Bury St. Edmunds is in spotting these distinctive names. Tremwade and Grimwade are ancient Suffolk names. So is Hilder, which is derived from an East Anglian name for the elder tree. Haylock, a name seldom found outside East Anglia and Essex, first appeared at Bury St. Edmunds in 1188 and has been common ever since. Pain, or Payne, from the Old French *paien*, meaning peasant or pagan in the rural sense of the word, is common in many counties; but it has been exceptionally common in East Anglia since the twelfth century, and in the thirteenth century it became common as a baptismal name. Another interesting feature of these old lists of local names is that they may provide clues to dialect variations which can be clues to original meanings. Whittle, for example, could mean white-well, or chalk-well; but as Whitwell in Cambridgeshire is still pronounced Whittle by natives, it seems reasonable to conclude that the Whittles in the Bury St. Edmunds list came from Whitwell in Cambridgeshire.

One of the most delightful Fenland names is Osler, 'wild fowler', from the Old French *oiseleur*. East Anglia, of course, is the wild fowler's paradise, which may well account for the surname Bird being common throughout the eastern counties south of the Wash, with the highest concentration in Norfolk. And in case someone is tempted to counter that Bird must be a common name everywhere, it is worth pointing out that for some obscure reason it is not. In few counties is it more than thinly distributed. Although fairly common in Gloucestershire, in Worcestershire it appears only as Byrd in old records. It is, in fact, as a result of Bird being a characteristically East Anglian name that it is now a New England name, especially common in Philadelphia. And while thinking of birds, it might be mentioned that the surname Coe, another East Anglian name, is the local form of the North Country surname Kay, which is derived from the Old Norse word for jackdaw, and that Diver has been a Cambridgeshire name for seven hundred years or more. Goose is incorporated in such typically Norfolk names as Gooseman, Gozzard, and Gazard—from goose-herd, and Negoose or Negus may have that source. On balance, however, they are more likely to be derived from the Old English *ecg*, 'corner', a word that gave rise to halls on the edge of parishes being called Egg Hall. Negus, on this argument would be *atten-egg-house*, 'us' being a common abbreviation of 'house'. My guess is that this is precisely what it is. Yet another curious East Anglian name is Rainbird, which Professor Weekley said was a dialect name for a woodpecker.

Scandinavian influences frequently enter into the reckoning in determining the origin of names in the coastal areas of Eastern England. Bond and Bundy are examples. Their obvious source would be bondsman; but they are more likely to be derived from the Old Norse *buande*, 'dwelling', a name given to a man who settled on a holding in order to cultivate the land: a husbandman. Scales is a related name that has had a home in East Anglia since the thirteenth century, appearing first as de Scales. Like the place-name, Scole, it is derived from the Scandinavian *skali*, 'a hut or temporary dwelling', which became Scale in Cumberland. Ketteridge, Tovell, Tuttle, Thirtle, Tovell are other anglicised Scandinavian names found mainly in East Anglia.

The vulnerability of the East Anglian coast, particularly in Suffolk, led to that suspicion of strangers which has always been a marked characteristic of the Suffolk character. This has sometimes been expressed through feigned misunderstanding by natives of what was either being said to them or asked of them. There are scores of Suffolk anecdotes illustrating this, many of them being elaborations of the basic exchange:

87

Traveller: 'Do you know the way to Bury?'
Villager, grinning broadly and walking away: 'I dew'.

No doubt this kind of experience by visitors to the county inspired the term 'silly Suffolk', which is grossly unfair, since Suffolk men usually know perfectly well what they are doing. They also know that they are more likely to accomplish it without interference if they keep their purpose to themselves. It is from this characteristic that we get the surname Pretty, which has nothing to do with beauty, but has its source in an Anglo-Saxon word meaning crafty or cunning, and no-one could deny that there is a substantial element of cunning in the Suffolk character. The original Mr. Prettyman may have been a local wizard, since that is the meaning of 'cunning man' in East Anglia. Silly in 'silly Suffolk', far from meaning foolish or weak-minded, is actually derived from an Anglo-Saxon word which became *sely*, and meant blissful or blessed.

Many Cambridgeshire surnames were introduced by men who came from the Low Countries to help with the draining of the Fens. There is a tradition at Willingham that the Jeeps family are descended from Dutchmen who came to work on the dykes. Gepp is a related name where it is not simply the pet form of Geoffrey, and Frohock is thought to have originated in the same way. A name we might not suspect of having any connection with the dykes is Half-penny, which had its origin in a mediaeval condition of tenure now largely forgotten. In Cambridgeshire it was kept alive through a levy imposed on certain lands for the repair of dykes. An instance of this is a piece of land at Elm, Cambridgeshire, called Halfpenny Field because tenants were required to contribute one half-penny per acre for the repair of Needham Dyke.

Names connected with agriculture are so common everywhere that there is no point in repeating them for each region; but local peculiarities can be clues to dialect surnames and local occupations. No doubt the first East Anglian Hackers made 'hacks', the old word for mattocks and hoes with which this rich land was brought into production when surnames were being orally acquired by the peasantry. Hackett is probably the same name; and we are tempted to add Hake despite Reaney's suggestion that it is from the fish. When we think of the vast areas of scrub and woodland that had to be cleared before the land could be prepared for cultivation, we may think it belonged to the Hacker group with Acket, Hackman, and Hackwood, which were clearly names borne by woodmen. But as Hackney, from an Old French word for an ambling horse, is certainly an exception, Hake may have been another.

A name from the same region which may be that either of a fisherman or of a woodcutter is Kiddy or Keddy, now an Essex name. It could be derived from 'kiddle', a weir in a river that was fitted with nets or wicker baskets to catch fish, or from *kidde*, 'faggot or bundle of sticks'. In Hertfordshire and the South Midlands we get the surname Bavin, originally given to a hedge-trimmer, or woodman who cut and sold faggots. The name comes from bavin, a bundle of four sticks bound with either one or two withies, which in some parts of England must have been applied to any bundle of brushwood, since Shakespeare, in *Henry IV*, refers to 'bavin wits'—wits that had a quick and short-lived blaze.

In regions where Scandinavian influence was strong we find many surnames derived from alders and ash trees. The explanation of this characteristic is that in Norse mythology the first man and the first woman were formed respectively from an ash tree and an alder tree. So in legends the ash, 'with its crown in heaven and its roots in hell' was the tree of life. A secondary effect of the prevalence of ash trees is the introduction of the surname Wainwright, which came because the steamed wood of the ash tree was found to be pliable and well adapted to wagon, or wain, making. Curiously, however, names ending in -wright, -maker, and -monger are comparatively rare in East Anglia. An odd exception is Dethewright, derived from an Old English word for tinder or fuel, which survives in truncated form as D'Eath or D'Aeth. Boatwright and Botwright, however, are fairly common names in Suffolk.

In a region as distinctive in character as East Anglia many surnames are sharply evocative. The Rushes, Reeders, and Thackers conjure up pictures of its reedy foreshore; the Fowlers, Iletts, Inces, and Ennises, its marshes and islets. In Essex we might be tempted to connect Musset with sea-fish; but if we did we should be mistaken. The name is derived from the bagpipes that the first holder of the name must have played before one of William's barons.

The insularity and peculiar character of the region make it more than usually unsafe to jump to conclusions unsupported by evidence. Shearman, Sherman, and Sharman are common surnames which might all be thought to be derived from the occupation name given to the man who sheared the nap off the cloth when the clothiers flourished here. In fact they are just as likely to have been given to a 'furriner' who came in from 'the Shires'. Nevertheless all the usual trade-names connected with the woollen industry are found in Norfolk and Suffolk—again with local peculiarities. Dexter and Lister are both Suffolk names for a dyer. It was a John Lister, dyer of Norwich, calling himself 'the king of the Commons', who led the 1381 rebellion. These -ster name endings are exceptionally common in East Anglia. They include Brewster, Webster, and Baxter, all found elsewhere; but not in my experience Throwster as an alternative to the common surname Thrower, which was the name given to the thread-thrower who converted raw silk into silk thread. As this, along with Threadgold for embroiderer, is found in the villages, there was clearly widespread luxury trade in the region at an early date.

Flemish weavers also brought into East Anglia a sprinkling of surnames not associated with trades. Many names ending in -kin, from the Dutch -ken, were introduced in this way. The common ending 'y' found in Jermy, Jarmy, and Jeremy are characteristic of this group. So is Joicey, which is spelt in at least eighteen different ways, and is believed to originate in the veneration of a saint who had a hermitage at *Josse-sur-mer*. Similarly, the French nickname *le enveise* or *envoisie*, 'playful, wanton', became Vaisey, Voysey, or Vesey. No doubt the ease with which a final 'y' or 'ey' slips off the tongue accounts for the popularity of this ending. It is probably because the great Norfolk family of Gurney, who came in at the Conquest from *Gournai-en-Brai*, had such an easy name for pronunciation that it has remained in uncorrupted form. The same reason must apply to Wansey, which came into East Anglia with Hugh de Waunci, who held the manor of Barsham under William the Conqueror.

The substitution of J for G, by which German became Jermin, or Jarmin, and Gerald became Jarrold, is typical of East Anglia, which in contrast to the West of England has a way of blurring consonants. Still more marked are the elisions. One of the most typical is that from 'house' to either 'us' or 'is' mentioned above in connection with Negus. The best known examples are the ever-willing Barkis in *David Copperfield*, whose name means 'barkhouse or tannery', Aldis and Aldous, which mean 'old house', and Windus, which means 'windhouse'. The exception is Challis, from Eschailes. I have heard this failure to enunciate clearly attributed to the force of the wind blowing the syllables back into the teeth of the man who utters them.

Alefounder, 'inspector of ale', is a curious name which survives in Essex and Norfolk. The second element in it is from the Latin *fundere* 'to pour out'. So an alefounder must have been the official appointed by the Court Leet to examine the ale as it was poured out. Catchpole is another intriguing East Anglian name. One theory is that it was borne by an under-sergeant who caught his victim with long wooden forceps that crossed on the delinquent's throat. Another is that it was the name of the official who collected the best hen—the *cache-poule*—for the lord of the manor or the rector of the parish in default of an obligatory payment. It is one of many East Anglian surnames that never will be finally agreed about, if only because the East Anglian is by nature a wag. Is Girling, for example, derived from coeur-de-lion, 'lion-heart', as some bearers of the name would have us believe, or is it, as Reaney suspected, related to Quodling and Quadling in Norfolk, and thence to the Codling apple, 'sound to the core'? But anyone who really wants to have fun with surnames, should cross the Stour into

Essex, where a landowner at Felsted and Rivenhall appears in Little Domesday as Roger *Deus Salvet Dominas*. He was known as Roger 'God-Save-the-Ladies', and the surname Godsave survives! One of Holbein's pictures includes a likeness of Thomas Godsalve, Registrar of the Consistory Court of Norwich. More cheerfully, Henry Drink-all-up is in a thirteenth-century list of Fines for Essex.

These are good fun, but more interesting to serious students of surnames are those which raise questions of Why or Wherefor, particularly names that have strayed from their original home. In the Norfolk Patent Rolls there is a complaint by Humfrey de Bohun, Earl of Hereford, that while he was absent in Wales on the king's business servants in his Norwich household were assaulted. Could these have been men he had brought over from the Marches who had incurred the wrath of the men of Norwich by being more successful than them with the ladies during their lord's absence? There was certainly a whole colony of Howells and Powells in Norfolk at the time.

The line of the de Bohun earls of Essex has disappeared. But although the de Bohuns have gone, the names of their servants and retainers still crop up. In 1248 the name John de Matham, from the Herefordshire village of Mathon under the Malvern hills—that is to say, from the country of the earldom already held by the de Bohuns—appeared in Essex, and the Mathams have outlived the de Bohuns in the county. Their name has continued in West Essex for seven hundred years, and made headlines in the National Press a few years ago when Arthur Matham of Chignal, who had worked on the same farm for sixty-one years, thatching the haystacks and being toasted Lord of the Harvest, showed fierce courage in fighting a fire in one of the stacks he had laboured to build. It is a joy to think that our modern enthusiasts for family history are at last bringing credit and renown to the Mathams no less than to the de Bohuns, de Veres, and de Mandevilles.

Despite this, as Essex is distinctively a manorial rather than an ecclesiastical county, it is to the records of the old landed families, most of whom have disappeared, that we must look for clues to origins of many early surnames. Horace Round[1] pointed out that the manorial character of Essex parishes is responsible for the large number of ancient family names used as suffixes to distinguish them: Mortimer, Ferrers, Walter, Basset, Peverel, Mandeville, Helion, Gernon, Mountfitchet, Virley, D'Arcy, Berners are a few of those that survive in the county today. What Horace Round meant was that among the counties of south-east England, Essex was distinctively the one in which the land was held from a lord, whereas in Kent there was gavelkind inheritance, and Suffolk was a region of small holdings cultivated by free tenants. This is why Suffolk villages so rarely preserve the names of their manorial lords. Instead, they bear the names of the saints to whom their parish churches are dedicated.

After suggesting that Prettyman probably originated in 'cunning man' it would be churlish not to mention the Essex family of Wiseman. It seems more than likely that their name had the same meaning as Prettyman. These small vernacular differences between names with the same meaning are an inexhaustible subject. Among the most respected Essex farming families is that of Goodchild, which has been an Essex name since the thirteenth century. In the Scandinavian counties to the north it became Goodbairn, Goodban, and even Goodband. The frequency of such names is surely evidence that the love and care of children is not something that came in with the Welfare State. Mott is another Essex name found in the west of the county since the thirteenth century that could be derived from a Scandinavian word meaning 'courage, vigour, might'; but it probably has its home at Mott Street in Epping Forest, where it means ditch or dyke in an embankment, in which case it is distinctively a local name. Other common names are localised by small peculiarities of spelling. Camp, for example, becomes Kemp hereabouts, with the diminutive Campkin peculiar to Hertfordshire. Dane in the Home Counties is more likely to be from *denu*, 'valley', than from the Scandinavian; but Danvers is neither. It is undoubtedly from de Anvers (Antwerp).

1. *Family Origins and Other Studies*, 1930

Three names that have excited my own interest as odd are Uncle, Living, and Daybell. Domesday was fortunately able to provide the clue to the first. It appears there as both Ulchel and Hunchel. Whether there was ever a pawnbroker with that surname or not I cannot say. The reason why Living seemed odd was its uselessness for purposes of identification, since the one thing we all have in common, if only temporarily, is that we are all alive to a greater or lesser degree. So I wondered whether, like D'Eath, it had a more complicated origin. As Loveling is an early name in Hertfordshire, it might be a related corruption, although another origin might occur to a wag who remembered that children born out of wedlock were sometimes referred to as 'love children'. As for Daybell, the name of a family of highly reputable solicitors, I accept Dr. Reaney's derivation of the name from a nickname conferred on an ancestor who was inclined to turn night into day, hence the couplet:

> *Thei daunsyd all the nyzt, till the son con ryse;*
> *The clerke rang the day-bell, as it was his gise.*

In other words, like the Poveys they were night birds!

Much of the beauty of this part of England is in the old wattle-and-daub cottages of its villages, now so lovingly preserved. So such trade names as Dauber are still found, while at the skilled end we have Pargeter. The eastern counties are as rich in old village names as they are in villages. When W. B. Gerish examined the records of the Hadham villages in Hertfordshire he found that Barker had been a local name since 1277, Brett and Cakebread since 1545. The second is interesting because it denotes a baker of cakes as distinct from a baker of bread. John, the cakebread man, who was asked to 'bake me a cake as fast as you can', was the man who produced what to us would be a sort of currant or spiced bread. Dellow, an early name in Much Hadham could be from de-le-hill, names retained by two old houses there. Gillett, a name that appears in Much Hadham parish registers from the beginning, is from a shortened form of Juliana that is the origin of Gillian and Jill, who may have gone 'up the hill' at Much Hadham to the houses of that name, although it would be an odd way to go in search of a pail of water unless there was a perennial spring up there, near which the houses were built.

In Essex we have one of the strangest names with a watery origin in Lippingwell or Leppingwell, which began as a place-name in Little Maplestead, and continues in corrupted form as a surname in the same part of the county. The name is traced by Dr. Reaney to an early holder; but he could have taken the name of a local well where the children practised leaping, or which the animals leapt. Another fascinating North Essex name is Tabor, from the old name for a drummer.

One of the most baffling surname problems is what happened to the many thousands of names of refugees from religious persecution on the Continent who settled in the eastern counties. The Huguenots have their historians, and scores of names of those who made their mark in England are proudly retained. Essex has some of the most distinguished, including the Bosanquets, Courtaulds, Crespignys, and Houblons. It seems probable that most of the poorer classes were absorbed into local life and took either the English equivalent of their original name or a more pronounceable corruption of it. In this way, Poisson would become Fish, and Fleur would become Flower. Many East Anglian and Essex names closely resemble Continental names. The Garretts could have been Gerards, the Garners could have been Gerners, from the Old French for 'storehouse for corn', or grainers. Certainly the Gernons took their name from a Frenchman who made himself conspicuous by wearing a moustache, which distinguished him from the majority of Normans, who were clean-shaven, so he was given a nickname that meant moustache.

The proximity of London has given the Home Counties an apparently unlimited range of Continental names. Many of them fluctuate between one county and another, particularly those derived from personal names, such as Rolph (from Rudolph) and Stacy (from Eustace). Some names reflect changes in local employment. Sworder, 'maker of swords', suggests an origin in Sussex, and it does appear there in the early iron-making days; but it has been established in Essex for hundreds of years, which might seem strange to anyone who does not know that Thaxted was the Sheffield of the Middle Ages.

With so many names circulating freely in Hertfordshire, Buckinghamshire and Bedfordshire it is interesting to single out names that have remained localised. In Buckinghamshire, names that may have started as Crook seem to have been modified to Croke. Perhaps Sir John Croke, who sleeps peacefully with his wife and eleven children represented on his tomb at Chilton, did not want to burden his family with an inherited name that might bring them under suspicion of deviousness! Abeare is a Hertfordshire surname that is only understood when we learn that it is a local dialect word for abide or abode. But the outstanding exception to surname mobility in the region is Bunyan, which has been a Bedfordshire name since 1204 and is found in no other county in early records. It has been noted in eleven forms in the parish of Elstow alone. Its origin is not *Bonjean*, 'good John', but the Old French *bugnon*, 'a raised knob', or bunion, which suggests something as physically uncomfortable as John Bunyan may have been spiritually uncomfortable to his own generation. Incidentally, the original meaning of Badman was not a man distinguished by wickedness, but beadsman, a man who prayed for others.

As we move away from London we find the number of long-established families increasing. The Botelers, 'makers of leather bottles', held the manor of Biddenham for three hundred and fifty years. The Conquests were at Houghton Conquest for five hundred years from 1223 to 1741. And what would Bedfordshire have been without the Whitbreads? They were at Gravenhurst in 1254, and since the days of Samuel Whitbread (1720–96) have been both munificent benefactors and far-sighted leaders of public life.

In Northamptonshire we find even more long-established families; but in many respects we are conscious of moving into closer association with the North Midlands than with the Home Counties. This was the county that Norden found so rich in gentle families that he called it 'the Herald's Garden'.

In Memory Of

JOHN CATCHPOLE
who died the 16ᵗʰ June 1787
Aged 75 Years.

My Horses have done Running.
My Waggon is decay'd,
And now in the Dust my Body is lay'd
My whip is worn out & my work It is done
And now I'm brought here to my last home.

1 Catchpole: an East Anglian
name that may have started
out as *cache-poule* (see p. 91).
A gravestone in Palgrave,
Suffolk

Sakings, now usually Sawkens —
possibly from *saul-kin*.
Intruded consonants are often
dialectical. This gravestone is at
Great Livermere, Suffolk

Here lieth y͏ͤ
body of William
Sakings he died
y͏ͤ 28ᵗʰ of march
1689 he was forkner
to King Charles y͏ͤ 1
King Charles y͏ͤ 2ᵈ
King James y͏ͤ 2ᵈ
Aged 78 Years

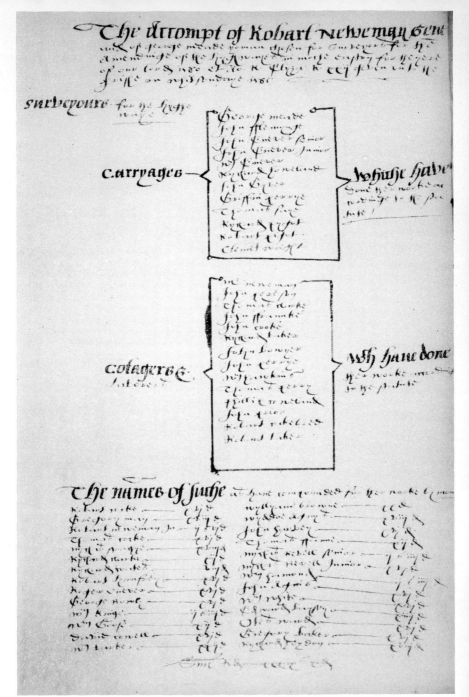

3 The 1581 Surveyor's Account for the repair of highways in the
parish of Great Easton, Essex

4 *opposite* Thaxted Hearth Tax, 1662

Bintul

Georgius Heydon	03
Johes Wright	01
Chapman vid	03
Arthur Burtini	01
Willus Slacke	02
	119

Raxtel

Thomas Smith Barronett	11
Johes Wright	02
Franciscus Howlett	04
Isaac Harris	01
Johes Piggott	01
Johes Everett	01
Ricus More	02
Willus ffranklyn	01
Ambrosius Sador	02
Johes Everod	01
Willus Buglock	01
Thomas Knapping	01
Willus Wrenn	02
Thos Sanders	01
Alexander Darby	01
Agnette Burling vid	01
Georgius Hawkins	02
Johes Salmon Cordwainer	02
Thomas Everord	02
Henricus Eve	02
Moses Everord	02
Georgius Henham	02
Johes Humfrey	06
Robtus ffann	07
Jacobus Goodday	03
Ricus Bouton	01
Thomas Porter	01
Jno ffarr	01
Josephus Westwood	01
Margeria Barber vid	01
Ricus Bauer	02
Ricus Porter	01
Thomas Claydon	04
Radus Purchas	01
Nathaniel Westley	04
Edrus Brookes	02
Jeronima Bird	03
Johes Wragg	01

Thaxted

Joshua Ragg	01
Jasper Powell	02
Thomas Wale	01
Johes Halls sen Downayner	03
Thomas Smith	03
Thomas Johnson	03
Thomas Derby gen	4
Thomas South	01
Elizabetha Westne vid	01
Susanna Ettenell vid	03
Thomas Pomfrett	03
Andreue ffith	03
Samuel Turner	03
Thomas Searle	01
Thomas Iuan	02
Jacobus Harris	03
Robtus Bartion	01
Willus Rich	03
Willus Darby	03
Thomas Shoppy	02
Robtus Spillman	04
Johes Poole	01
Robtus Neale	05
Robtus Neale	01
Johes Raynor	06
Elizabetha Wood vid	03
Thomas Clarke	02
Jno Barford	01
Maria Westly	02
Benjamin Pory	06
Xpofer Turner	06
Samuel ffann	04
Abrahus Harris	01
Willus Turner	06
Leond Badcocke	02
Johes Chapman	01
Johes Hallo de Stanbrooke	03
Maria Wales vid	04
Ricus Croute	04
Willus Dorrell	03
Johes Stubberfeild	02
Willus Poole	01
Thomas Harris Senior	01
Edrus Morrell	03
Margaret Clarke vid	03

Apothecary (see pp. 15–16)

Brazier (see p. 16)

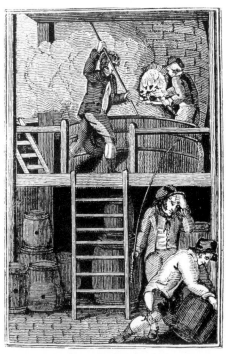

Brewer (see p. 90)

Cutler (see p. 102)

Dyer (see p. 55) Tanner (see p. 56)
Turner (see pp. 16, 21) Weaver (see pp. 17, 55, 71)

5 Occupations from which surnames have developed, as illustrated in
the *Book of English Trades and Library of the Useful Arts* (London, 1823)

Parish of Dunmow Hundred

N° of Cert.	Date	Persons Names	Description	N° of Cert.	Date	Persons Names	Description
		Barnston				**Dunmow Great,** continued	
62	May 5	Burton John	Housekeeper	4	May 16	Clubbe Charles	Hous.ᵈ
63	June 1	Simpson Jane	Sister	5	16	Do Catherine	Wife
33	May 25	John Revd Nicholas	Hous.ᵈ	15	19	Doones Mary	Serv.ᵗ
34	25	Do Mary	Wife	6	16	Edwards Joseph	Hous.ᵈ
46	June 1	Wood Stephen	Hous.ᵈ	7	16	Do Ann	Wife
47	1	Do Sarah	Wife	23	20	Hoakes Benjamin	Hous.ᵈ
				13	19	Gunn John	Do
				24	21	Howlett Revd John	Do
		Braxted		25	20	Do Sarah	Wife
158	June 5	Leader Ann	Wife of The?	53	June 2	James John	Hous.ᵈ
159	5	Do Ann	Daur	54	2	Do Mary	Wife
61	5	Seabine Martha	Lodger	32	May 25	Lowe Melicent	Hous.ᵈ
21	May 20	Stock Edward	Hous.ᵈ	9	16	Lukin Tom	Do
22	20	Do Rebecca	Wife	27	21	Meister Isaac	Do
				28	21	Do Mary	Wife
				31	23	Parsons George Clubbe	Serv.ᵗ
		Canfield Great		1	16	Pearson Richard	Lodger
30	June 3	Mooton Revd Robt Lewes	Hous.ᵈ	2	16	Do John junr	Serv.ᵗ
				3	16	Do William	Do
				45	June 1	Perkins Elizabeth	Do
		Canfield Little		8	May 16	Oben Revd John Christian	Hous.ᵈ
40	May 30	Barnard Thomas	Hous.ᵈ	66	June 5	Philbrick Samuel	Do
41	30	Do Ann	Serv.ᵗ	10	May 18	Rayner John	Do
36	June 3	Butterfield Revd James	Hous.ᵈ	11	18	Do Sarah Feeney	Wife
				19	20	Scruby John	Hous.ᵈ
				20	20	Do Sarah	Wife
		Dunmow Great		57	June 3	Do James	Hous.ᵈ
26	May 21	Barnard John	Hous.ᵈ	17	May 19	Jones Revd Benjamin	Lodger
44	30	Do Ann	Serv.ᵗ	49	June 2	Smith William	Son of St
2	28	Bradbury Mary … Mary		39	May 29	Do Sarah	Daur
		Do Sarah	Daurs of The above	12	18	Sole Susannah	Serv.ᵗ
		Do Amy		35	24	Toke Nicholas	Lodger
54	19	Bridge Thomas	Hous.ᵈ	16	19	Wade George	Hous.ᵈ
12	30	Clapton Ann	Do				
13	30	Do Mary	Do				
68	June 24	Do Eliz.ᵗʰ Ann	Daur of A.			*(Continued)*	
69	24	Do John	Son of A.				

6   Certificates for using hair powder issued for the year 1795

146 S.

Persons Convicted	Abode	Occupat.n	Offences	N.o
George Silvester	Hatfield Broad oak	Lab.r	Unlawfully having an Hare in his Custody	
Do	Do	Do	Keeping & using a Snare for the destruction of Game not being qualified	
Sarah the Wife of Arthur Sayer	Waltham Holy Cross	Do	Having in her possion. a bundle of Wood & not giving a satisfactory acct. thereof	1.
John Smith	Barking	Do	Having in his posses.n wood & Underwood without legal right	
Robert Stringfellow	Great Wakering	Shop Keeper	Selling or Exposing to Sale British Thread Lace without licence	
William Spurgin	Hatfield Peverel	Farmer	Keeping & using a Gun & Dog to kill Game not being qualified	
Thomas Shore	Enfield Middx.	Gent.	Keeping & using a Gun at Nazeing not being qualified	
William Stedman	Chigwell	Chimney Sweeper	Having in his possion. a bundle of Wood & not giving a satisfactory account how he came by the same	1.
John Squires	Loughton	Labourer	a like offence	1.
Ann Siggins	High Laver	Singlewoman	a like offence	1.
Elizabeth the Wife of Edward Sapsworth	Great Hallingbury	Labourer	a like offence	1.
Susan the Wife of Abraham Sapsworth	Do	Do	a like offence	1.
Mary Sapsworth	Do	Spinster	a like offence	1.
Thomas Futters	—	—	For having assaulted & abused Thomas Stonyball the Governor of the Workhouse of Chappel	

7 Summary convictions and sentences, 1818–19, reflecting the high proportion involving poaching

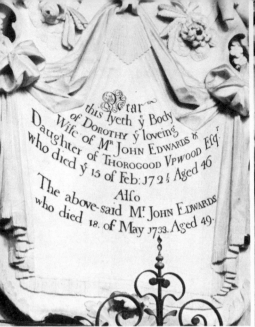

8   The interest of the Edwards monument at Terrington St Clements, Norfolk, is in Thorogood which probably originated in the Scandinavian *Thorgott*, 'Thor-Geat', as the 'gates' in York

9   Bovey (Cheam, Surrey) from a river-name in Devon. River-names are common in the South West

10   Finch (St Mary the Great, Cambridge) with an origin suggested in Finch Lane, London

CHAPTER SIX

Lincolnshire and the North Midlands

It could probably be said with accuracy that the proportion of Lincolnshire surnames almost entirely confined to the county at the beginning of the present century was as high as thirty *per cent*. Many of them are readily traceable to Scandinavian place-names, reminding us that it was in Lincolnshire that Viking settlement reached its peak. The vast majority of these local surnames end in -by, with such corruptions as Sotheby from Southby. To a lesser extent this Scandinavian characteristic continues throughout the North Midlands, with Nott for Cnut and Swane for Svein, and where innumerable names end in -by, of which the best known are Digby, Thoresby, and Orby from Lincolnshire; Gadsby, Hoby, and Kilby from Leicestershire; Willoughby from the three counties of Lincolnshire, Leicestershire and Nottinghamshire, and the ubiquitous Kirby, which is common to all counties of Scandinavian settlement. The most interesting of these locative surnames from the historian's point of view are those in which Scandinavian and Anglian elements are combined. These suggest either places in which there was happy co-existence, or those in which there was already an established name from an earlier culture when the Vikings arrived.

Anglo-Scandinavian names are an interesting study. One that might not be suspected of such an origin, Kilvert, actually began as Ketilfrith, which contains the Norse *ketil* (cauldron) element, found also in Ankill. This combination of 'An' and 'ketil' or 'ketel', found originally in the Lincolnshire surname, Anketell, and in corrupted form in Ankin, Antin, Annakin and Annikin, was introduced by the Normans from parts of France where Norse influence had been active. As the root from which we get our 'kettle' is found in so many languages from the Icelandic to the Dutch, the numerous corruptions are not surprising. Tuck and Maw (from sea-mew) are other Anglo-Scandinavian names that have their home along the east coast north and south of the Wash, and among the descriptive names that are so often characteristic of Scandinavian influence there is the curious Lincolnshire surname Wroot, which started as a place-name meaning 'snout', so must have been chosen as descriptive of a spur of land resembling a pig's snout. We shall find similar names when we reach Norse Cumbria.

This individuality of Lincolnshire surnames makes them all the more notable when they turn up in other counties. Dr. Reaney records eight generations of the Spalding family following the craft of carpenter as freemen of York. There can never be any doubt about the racial origin of Spalding; but descriptive surnames frequently beg questions if the first recorded appearance is not prefixed by 'de'. An instance of this is Rigby, which is now prolific in Lancashire. As it means 'dweller in the farm on the ridge' it could occur wherever 'Rigg' is the local form of 'Ridge'; but with the prefix 'de' it is safe to assume that it originated in the Lincolnshire village of Rigsby.

In looking at East Anglian names we noted that many of them came from Yorkshire. They are quite as common in Lincolnshire—most notably in Tennyson, which means 'son of Denis', with the typical Yorkshire substitution of 't' for 'd'. The Tennysons were related to the Rawnsleys, who also came from Yorkshire. Both these clerical and literary families showed great affection for the county of their adoption and appreciation of its distinctive character, although I always feel that there is a strong Yorkshire element in Tennyson's *Northern Farmer*. However that may be, his 'haunt of ancient Peace' was Gunby, the home of the Massingberd family, who had been in Lincolnshire since the fourteenth century and boasted a name found nowhere else.

Fenland names found south of the Wash continue in Lincolnshire. Ducker and Duckering remain common; but what at first sight looks odd is that names introduced by the Dutchmen who came over to drain the Fens are much less frequent in Lincolnshire than in Cambridgeshire. The reason for this must lie somewhere in the way in which the draining of the Lincolnshire Fens was accomplished by the 1st Earl of Lindsay. The Dutch names that are found, such as Colcheeper, from Koolschipper (collier), are largely confined to the bulb fields. No doubt many names that came into the county from overseas were absorbed and anglicised. When we remember what happened to the simple name Hugh, the name of two Lincoln saints and the source of up to ninety surnames in the county, we cannot be surprised that surname origins can as easily be lost in Lincolnshire as a man can be lost on its fens.

Some of these corruptions may have arisen from the kind of cunning we noted in Suffolk, and it is tempting to suggest that the Lincolnshire surname Prettyjohn is the local form of the Suffolk Prettyman, meaning 'cunning man or wizard'; but the scholars have a different source, which may itself be no more than an instance of local cunning. Anyway, the story goes that the name was originally Prestreiohan, the name of a priest-king who ruled over a territory in Central Asia in the twelfth century and won renown by a victory over the Medes and Persians. Between 1165 and 1177 a forged letter purporting to be from him circulated in Europe and eventually reached Lincolnshire, where the name of the priest-king was given to a child who grew up to be an attorney. *Prester John*, it will be remembered, was the name of a novel by John Buchan.

Lincolnshire has its full share of romantic stories connected with its landed families, although we may be struck by the number of names that clearly originated elsewhere, sometimes in apparently unrelated places. The Dymokes of Scrivelsby Court appear to take their name from Dymock in Gloucestershire; but as the etymology of Dymock is obscure the link does not provide a clue to the origin of the family name. The interest in the family is that its head is hereditary Grand Champion of England, an office conferred by William the Conqueror on a favourite into whose family the Dymokes married. The original holders held Tamworth Castle 'by service of coming to the king's Coronation, armed cap-à-pie with Royal Arms delivered by the king, seated on the Sovereign's chief charger and offering himself in combat against anyone opposing the Coronation'. The right to hold Scrivelsby in this manner by Grand Serjeanty was disputed in the fourteenth century; but an Inquisition in 1332 confirmed the claim that it was held 'by finding on the day of the king's Coronation an armed knight on horseback to prove by his body, if necessary, against whomsoever challenges that the king who is crowned on that day is the true and rightful heir to the kingdom'. It is now kept alive by the carrying of the Royal Standard at a Coronation.

It is reasonable to suppose that many of the Becks and Beks in Lincolnshire take their name from the Old Norse word for a stream, while in the heavily wooded Dukeries inland we need to bear in mind the Old English word *becca*, 'mattock', no doubt derived from the action of a bird's beak, which probably inspired the invention of the tool. The patrician family bearing the name claim to derive it from Bec in Normandy; but it is not impossible that even with them it comes down from an ancestor who had a prominent nose, or beak, so was given the surname as a nickname. In any case, there are several places called Bec in France, and *bec* is an Old French word for bill or beak. The Norman family of Bek in Lincolnshire split early into three branches, the Beks of Eresby, the Beks of Luceby, and the Beks of Botheby. Anthony Bek, who died in 1310, son of Walter of Eresby, became bishop of Durham. For defying Edward I he was deprived of his temporalities, but after the Pope's intervention these were restored to him and he was granted the sovereignty of the Isle of Man by Edward II. Anthony Bek (d. 1343) of the Luceby line became bishop of Norwich. Thomas, the elder brother of the first Anthony was chancellor of Oxford University, and a second Thomas, son of the second Anthony, was bishop of Lincoln.

When we move into the Dukeries we get the question that intrigues so many overseas visitors as to why several noble titles have no recognisable connection with the estates of those who hold them. The strangest of these is found in Derbyshire, where the title of Duke of Devonshire is held by the head of the Cavendish family from a village in Suffolk! It would not be a profitable exercise here to explain this particular idiosyncracy of the English nobility; but extra-regional surnames borne by so many of the gentry are worth mentioning. A good starting point for the study of these would be the lists of the county magistracy during the Civil War. They would provide clues to political reasons for changes in family fortunes. But not all the families that suffered during the Civil War had been long in possession of their estates, and some who lost them under Cromwell regained them under Charles II. Nevertheless, these lists provide broad clues to the social changes that became marked in the Midlands at this time, as Industry developed and those who made money by it put their profits into land and bought themselves status.

The creation of the order of baronetcy by James I had led to the foundation of many landed families, drawn either from yeoman farming stock or from manufacturing families. The Paget family, whose name became associated with the marquisate of Anglesey, first made their money as nail-makers in Wednesbury. Perhaps the best evidence of this social movement is to be found on the sumptuous monuments to members of newly enriched families in parish churches. A tour of those in Leicestershire with this in mind would produce such names as Appleby, Hastings, Villiers, Grey, Gifford, Nevill, Brudenell and many more, all borne by families whose roots were in other counties. This does not, however, imply that Leicestershire lacks ancient families. Purefoy was a Leicestershire name in the reign of Henry III, and Beaumont is a Conquest name that Wordsworthians delight to honour.

But in the North Midlands we again find that the most rewarding searches are into names closely related to the earth from which they sprang. There are many of them still. Howitt is a corruption of 'hew-it' and conjures up visions of woodland being cleared. Stubbins is a related name, and Carver might be said to complete the process. Other forestry names in this land of forests are Hardstaff, common in Sherwood, and Collingwood, a Staffordshire surname meaning 'the wood of disputed ownership', while Wilber is a corruption of 'wild-boar'. Many others could be extracted from Directories; but the one that some of us will always esteem above the rest in Leicestershire is Herrick, borne by the family that gave us the poet of Dean Prior in Devonshire and Dean Swift, whose father married into it and who wrote of the Herricks: 'There is a tradition that the most ancient family of Ericks derive lineage from Erick the Forester, a great commander, who raised an army to oppose the invasion of William the Conqueror, by whom he was vanquished, but afterwards employed to command that prince's forces, and in his old age retired to his house in Leicestershire, where his family hath continued ever since'. Heyrick is a variant of the name. A Mrs. Heyrick of Leicester, who died in 1611 at the age of ninety-seven, left one hundred and forty-two descendants. So it is no wonder that the name should still be found there.

In *The Midland Peasant,* Professor W. G. Hoskins traces the continuity of local families in the village of Wigston Magna in Leicestershire, giving life to dull dates from the thirteenth century onwards by associating them with names to be read on shop-signs, and borne by villagers still to be found tilling the land in the parish: Molds, Vanns, and Pawleys. He shows how surnames were established there in the second half of the thirteenth century and speculates on the origin of the Randolfs and Randulls, whose names might be derived from a Norwegian ancestor named Ranulfr, 'shield-wolf'. It is an exercise we could all repeat in our own parishes, and discover unsuspected romance in common names, as also in such curious names as two that appear to be peculiar to Staffordshire: Caterbanck, which might be thought to anticipate Common Market stockpiling, and many that seem to originate in Fernyhough, 'the ferny hollow'.

In the Black Country we find again names first encountered in Sussex, such as Bloomer and Glazier. Cutler inevitably occurs, along with Bowler, which must have started with a long-forgotten maker or seller of bowls—a forerunner of

Josiah Wedgwood. Homer is there, from *le Heaumer,* a maker or seller of helmets, and his sub-contractor, Rivett, the man who drove rivets into armour. The Salts have been there since the thirteenth century. Even the great Staffordshire family of Biddulph take their name from a place that means 'by the mine', or *dulf,* and Buddle, the name given to the man who washed the ore, is also there.

Cockin, a Midlands name that first appeared in Nottingham in the thirteenth century, is interesting in that it may be linked with Cokinbred, a Leicestershire name for a baker of cocket-bread, which was leavened bread slightly inferior to that baked of the finest flour. If this is right, Mr. Cockin would do business with Mr. Detheridge, a rare name surviving in Staffordshire and Essex from an Old English word for fuel or tinder, which was no doubt borne by a log-seller. And may it not be that it was because so many Black Country occupations were thirsty work that this became brewers' country? There is certainly no doubt about the connection of the Midlands with brewing. The old local name Cadman means 'a maker of casks, or framer of casks or barrels', and it is hardly surprising that another North Midlands surname, Godber, should be said to be a shortened form of good-beer, although it is, in fact, a contraction of God-be-here, which probably arose as a salutation: 'God be in this house', a much more gracious salutation than the Sussex surname: Gotobed!

A good instance of dialect variations is the North Midlands 'Hurt',—identical in origin with Hertfordshire's 'Hert', and Bedfordshire's 'Hart'—which is found also in Warwickshire and Norfolk. There was the landowning family named Hurt at Ashbourne from which sprang the Hurts of Kniveton, Casterne, and Alderwashley. The name also occurs in Lincolnshire. Such variations show again how slipshod our ancestors were with vowels. At the same time, when we find such a name as Wetherall acquiring eleven different spellings along a broad belt between the Welsh border and East Anglia, we might suspect a source far removed from the region. If we did we should be right. It means the haugh where the wethers are kept, and is derived from a place-name in Cumberland. Heathcote is a place-name in Derbyshire and Warwickshire, where it is pronounced as one would expect; but in Epping Forest we have the Boothby-Heathcotes, who pronounce their name Hethkett, the pronunciation adopted by the Yorkshire Heathcotes.

The Staffordshire family of Haden could provoke all the problems so frequently associated with the 'den' ending, which are increased rather than diminished in the North Midlands by the presence of the Cheshire river name, Dane. The innocent-at-large might think High Haden looked rather like High Halden in Kent, where the 'den' was a swine pasture. The two are quite unrelated. Nor is Haden related to Haldane, the surname that means 'half-dane', nor yet to Dane End in Hertfordshire, which means 'valley end' from *denu*, 'valley'. The vowels 'a' and 'e' are all too readily interchangeable in this part of the country, as we know from Derby the city, producing Darby the surname. Happily, Haden has been a Staffordshire name since the Conquest, so there is ample documentation to provide a clue to its meaning. The first references are to *atte Hauden*, or *de la Haude*, so we may be reasonably sure that the name means 'a wooded rise'. The Haden family owned property at Rowley Regis for six hundred years. Adenbroke, or Addenbrooke, which began as *de Adenbrok* and is now associated with the great hospital at Cambridge, is apparently a related name.

While looking at the dos and don'ts of the dens and the danes, it is worth mentioning that the River Dane produced the surname Davenport, in which 'port' does not mean harbour but market town, as it does in some Newports and Bridports. In view of there being so many areas for dispute in the pedigrees of names and families, it was perhaps understandable that the Erdeswicke family had their family tree painted on the walls of the thirteenth-century church at Sandon in Staffordshire.

In Derbyshire we move out of the woodlands of the Dukeries into a region in which surnames can usually be established with a greater degree of certainty. Topographical features again become safe clues to identity, particularly in the Peak, where woods are smaller and confined to the dales, and where there are few minor streams, because the limestone is permeable and does not require the surface drainage essential in clay country. Settlement on the well-drained uplands was therefore early, as it was in Wiltshire. So we have hill-forts, earthworks, and stone circles, while tree names are found, as they were on Exmoor, because they were rare and distinctive enough to be landmarks. Ashbourne, for example, means 'the stream where the ash trees grew'. The many Ashbys in the North Midlands show how important the ash tree—found especially on outcrops of mountain limestone—must have been. It provided valuable food for deer in autumn. So did the alder in autumn and the holly in winter, with the result that we get the Derbyshire name Ollerenshaw, which means alder wood, while Renshaw, another Derbyshire name which seems to be incorporated in the longer one, means Ravenshaw, itself a Derbyshire surname. These woods were found useful to peg-makers. So we get the local name Pegge, which alternatively, of course, may be from the pet name for Margaret. The Ashbourne Pegges endowed almshouses and left money for the poor. They served as High Sheriff and in the Rev. Samuel Pegge of Whittington produced an antiquary of note. The 'Hollin' ·names that are so numerous in Derbyshire and Cheshire in the various forms that include Hollingworth, Hollingshead, and Hollingshed, are usually from the holly tree; but they can be from hollow or hole.

Topographical names abound in Derbyshire. Beresford is a name with a long pedigree at Stoke-on-Trent. Tansley is a local surname derived from a place-name meaning 'valley branching off from the main dale', so it is a name that could only be found in this kind of country. Haddon, another name peculiar to Derbyshire, means 'heather-covered hill'. Repton is a tribal name. It means the hill of the Hrype tribe. One of the oldest Derbyshire names is Dethick, 'death oak', a name acquired from proximity to the tree from which felons fell to their death and remained for public display as a warning. There is a place with this name near Matlock, which means 'moot-oak', so the journey from Matlock to

Dethick was the Derbyshire equivalent of the London journey to Tyburn.

Fortunately many place-names that became surnames evoke pleasanter pastoral scenes. Ramsley and Tupton remind us of the immemorial use of these uplands for sheep grazing. Calver was the ridge where the calves were grazed; Calton Lees was where they were reared. Swanwick was the 'wick' or farm of the swineherds. But Cowley cannot be 'cow pasture' in Derbyshire as it is in Gloucestershire, because it first appears as Col-leah, which means 'clearing where charcoal was burnt', and the surname derived from this place-name is still pronounced Colley. Hathersage, ten miles from Sheffield, is a valley under the shadow of Millstone Edge in which the first part of the name is from the Old English word for the he-goat, so this was a place where goats were reared. As the surname derived from the place takes a large variety of forms including Athersuch, Athersych, Atherstytch, Hathersich and Athersedge, it seems probable that the goat-herds who travelled from pasture to pasture carried the name with them, transferring it orally from one place to another.

Alsop-en-le-Dale has produced one of the best known and most prolific Derbyshire families, spelling their name in forms ranging from Allsop, through Allsep to Elsep, with the family firm at Burton giving it the most familiar variant. It is a name that has been in Derbyshire since Domesday. The Derbyshire surnames Tideswell, Tiddswell, and Tidsale are all from the place-name Tideswell, which tends to be pronounced Tidza locally, so in this case the corruptions are dialectical and understandable. Some of these Derbyshire names are so obscure in origin that we should be grateful that they have been recast in more comprehensible forms if scholars would not persist in tracing them back to their roots! Shawcross is an example. What could be simpler than a cross in a wood as a means of identification. But we are told that the surname is derived from Shacklecross, which plunges us into all the problems associated with the Shackerleys in Lancashire, in which the first part is said to be from an Old English word meaning 'robber', and may even involve us in the problems over the meaning of Shakespeare's name, which could be associated with armed robbery!

Few of the Danish names found in eastern England persist into Derbyshire, which Scandinavians reached from the west, not the east. Most of them were Norwegians, and belonged to the Norse shepherd stock we shall meet in Cumbria who reached England from Ireland. On landing, some of them turned south and found in the Peak a countryside as much to their liking as their kinsmen were to find on the fells of Westmorland. It is from them that we find such names in Derbyshire as Copeland, which means 'bought land', Stanton, and Slack, from the Old Norse word for a shallow valley. And just as we found Sayce, meaning Saxon, in Shropshire for the odd man out, in Derbyshire we find Bretton, which indicates British survival in a Scandinavian region.

A name that seems to me to pose special problems in Derbyshire and the North of England is Lister. We met it in the South as the occupation name for a dyer. I doubt whether this will be accepted as the origin of their name by the descendants of John Lyster de Derby, who lived in the time of Edward II and was reputed to be the son of Sir Thomas Lyster de Derby. Many of the descendants of John Lyster now spell their name with 'i' substituted for 'y'; but most of them are of the 'Midhope' stock, which reached nobility in Lord Ribblesdale of Gisburn Park in the West Riding of Yorkshire, the subject of Sargent's finest portrait. Occurring at so early a date in Derbyshire, the name is probably from the Norse word for spear-head, or salmon spear, from which is derived Lyster Fiord, near Christiana, and the term 'lystering', used in the North of Scotland and elsewhere for salmon-spearing. Bagshaw is another Derbyshire name with alternative meanings. It could be 'badger wood'; but again it could have a Scandinavian origin. It could be from *bagge*, 'wether ram'.

The most remarkable name of French origin in Derbyshire is Foljambes, now surviving as Fulljames. It is made up of two words, *fol*, 'foolish', and *jambe*, 'leg', suggesting a nickname given to a man with a maimed or useless limb. Tombs of members of this family are to be seen in the south chapel of the church with the crooked spire at Chesterfield. The better-known name of French origin, Peveril, has now disappeared, although formerly found from Norman times in Warwickshire, Huntingdonshire, Middlesex and Essex. This also began as a nickname for a small man with a fiery temper, derived from the French word for pepper.

Tombs in Derbyshire churches remind us of many other great Derbyshire families. At Hathersage we see the arms of the Eyres entwined with those of the Padleys on the octagonal font, celebrating the union of two families early in the fifteenth century. The Eyres are among the oldest of Derbyshire families. Joan Eyre built the church at Stoney Middleton as a thank-offering for the safe return of her husband from Agincourt. Like the Shirleys (bright clearing), the Eyres bear a name not exclusively associated with Derbyshire, the county in which both have long and honourable records. It would be foolish to say much about such families except where they are uniquely localised, which for our purpose usually means where they bear a local place-name as surname, or have given their surname to a place. Having said that, the Babingtons spring to mind as a family whose name figures whenever the story of Mary, Queen of Scots is retold.

Any reference to the Shirleys tends to bring back to mind the lines about 'The glories of our blood and state' being 'shadows, not substantial things'. Derbyshire has one of the strangest of these stories. It is told by Sir Bernard Burke in his *Vicissitudes of Families*. Findern, near Derby, a name that means 'wood-house', was the home for nine generations from the reign of Edward I to that of Henry VIII of a family of that name, members of which distinguished themselves in the Crusades, at Crecy, and at Agincourt, while at home they served as Rangers of Needwood Forest and Castellans of Tutbury. They had their memorials in the church at Findern, but so complete was their eclipse that when Sir Bernard Burke, as Ulster King of Arms, went in search of evidence of this once great family he found not a trace of the hall they had lived in, and not a single memorial surviving in the church. But when a villager was asked if the name meant anything to him, he replied: 'Findernes? We have no Findernes here; but we have something that once belonged to them: we have Finderne flowers', and Sir Bernard was shown a bank covered with wild flowers that Sir Geoffrey Finderne had introduced from the Holy Land.

Cheshire may be too proud a county to think of itself as being in the Midlands; but its most distinguished inhabitants could hardly object to the local links with the oldest of all our families, the Ardens of Warwickshire, being brought in. The Ardernes have been a Cheshire family since the thirteenth century; but whether or not they are linked conclusively with the pre-Conquest Ardens may be open to question. The name begs many of the questions already mentioned in connection with the name 'Dane', and these questions increase as we move northward into country with very different racial traditions from those of the South of England. When we reach the North Riding of Yorkshire, the first syllable of Arden could be *earn*, 'eagle', or *ear*, 'gravel', and we should have to look for a clue to the meaning of the second syllable, which is presumably *denu*, 'valley'. In Cheshire, we are assured, eagles and gravel are both to be dismissed from the reckoning since early appearances of the name indicate that it is derived from *earderne*, 'dwelling-house'. It may be thought that this suggests that the genealogical approach to the subject of surnames may be more helpful than the philological. If so, Cheshire is our county, since as Camden said in *Britannia*, it 'is the great nursing-mother of the gentry; for there is no other English county that formerly supplied the king's army with more nobility, or that could number more knightly families'. And those knightly families, as we know from many sources, tended to intermarry because, according to Fuller in *The Worthies*, by choosing their wives near home they knew the stock they came from and were less likely to go wrong.

Fuller may have been right in this; but we may be surprised to find him adding that such intermarriages 'have been both a prolonger of worshipful families, and a preserver of amity between them'. A local proverb suggests a different effect of intermarriage:

> *Cheshire born and Cheshire bred*
> *Strong in the arm and weak in the head.*

However, this may not apply to the sort of families Fuller had in mind. He goes on to mention the Starkies, the Savages of Macclesfield, and the Suttons of Prestbury, whose head, Sir Richard Sutton, was the first lay founder of Brasenose, and the Cholmondeleys, who proliferated into other counties as Chumleys, Chumbleys, Chamleys, Chambleys, while the patrician stock kept the original name (from Ceolmund's ley) but made a concession over the pronunciation and called themselves Chumley. This pronunciation is no more an affectation than the Mainwaring pronunciation 'Mannering', or the Marjoribanks 'Marshbanks'. These and many other families have simply adopted common usage for the ordinary social exchanges of life, while retaining the original form as evidence of inheritance. So if there is any snobbery involved, it is in retaining the ancient form of the name, not in adopting the form in common use for pronunciation.

Camden's reference to knightly families which sprang to the king's aid reminds us of a passage in Drayton's *Polyolbion*, which gives a very different view from Fuller's about these intermarrying families living in amity together. It occurs in his description of the bloody battle fought between Henry IV and Hotspur Percy.

> *There Dutton, Dutton kills; a Done doth dill a Done;*
> *A Booth, a Booth; and Legh by Legh is overthrown;*
> *A Venables against a Venables doth stand,*
> *A Troutbeck fighteth with a Troutbeck hand to hand:*
> *Then Molineux doth make a Molineux to die;*
> *And Egerton the strength of Egerton doth try.*
> *O Cheshire, wert thou mad, of thine own native gore*
> *So much until this day thou never shed'st before.*

The Venables, who took their name from a place in Normandy, continued in direct line until 1679 and were the last survivors of the original barons of Cheshire. From the Duttons sprang the Warburtons, whose crest is a Saracen's Head, in allusion to the occasion when a Warburton vanquished a Saracen in combat. Their name is from a place in Cheshire, as also is the name of the Stathams, who are descended from a Norman Constable of Chester Castle, but for 350 years were most numerous in the Derbyshire dales. When we look at the rest of the list we may agree that Fuller was certainly right when he referred to the prolonging of worshipful families in Cheshire. There is the other rhyme that goes:

> *As many Leighs as fleas, Massies as asses,*
> *Crewes as crows, and Davenports as dogs' tails.*

The patrician 'Leighs' spell their name Legh, and in looking through a guide to the county I found Leghs seated in nine places, Masseys in five, Crewes in seven, and Davenports in ten. The Davenports have an even more sinister crest than the Warburtons. It is a rogue's head with a halter round the neck. In the Royal Forest of Macclesfield they had power of life and death over intruders and offenders against Forest laws. The Leghs continue to serve the county with candour and distinction. They claim descent from Edward de Lega, or Legh, who lived in the time of William II. Some of these families appear to have moved from one place to another as the result of marriages with neighbours. Dunham Massey, for example, passed from the Masseys to the Booths. And in mentioning the Duttons and the Masseys, we must not forget the Worthingtons, whose name, however, comes from Lancashire. Nor are these the only families between which alliances have continued for centuries. So it is little wonder that it used to be said to anyone planning a visit to Cheshire: 'Be careful what you say. Remember, they are all cousins'.

CHAPTER SEVEN

Lancashire and Yorkshire

It is all too easy for Lancashire comedians to produce jokes about such surnames as Higginbottom, Shufflebottom, or Ramsbottom for club audiences who have never heard that 'bottom' means 'shallow valley' in Lancashire, Cheshire, and probably Northumberland, since Percy Hotspur in Henry IV, Part I, Act iii, has the lines,

> *It shall not wind with such a deep indent,*
> *To rob me of so rich a bottom here.*

Nor would their audiences know that 'higgin' is a dialect word for both 'oaken' and the mountain-ash, that Shufflebottom is a wag's corruption of the Lancashire place-name, Shipperbottom, and that Ram is not only the name of the male sheep, but also a local name for wild garlic, which grows profusely in Ram's Wood, Haslingden, near Ramsbottom. This origin is, in fact, supported by the great naturalist, John Ray, who believed that Ramsey took its name from the plant.

Lancashire and Yorkshire are beyond all others the counties of local dialects which, pronunciation apart, have produced a host of surnames of doubtful origin, even to scholars. Geldard, a common name in Lancashire, could be either goat-herd or swineherd, since 'galt' is a local word for pig. Whitaker could be white-acre, wheat-acre, or wet-acre. Even as apparently simple a surname as Baines could be 'bones' if it started in Scotland; 'straignt or direct', from the Old Norse *beinn*, if it started in the North-East; or 'bath', from the French *bain*, if it started in the South. All three were examined by the distinguished branch of the family that produced Edward Baines, writer of topographical books at the beginning of the nineteenth century, Matthew Talbot Baines, Chancellor of the Duchy of Lancaster in the middle of the century, and his son, Thomas, who published histories of Lancashire, Cheshire, and Yorkshire.

We can imagine how these names baffled the French clerks who first recorded them from the lips of dalesmen whose speech was unintelligible to them anyway. So it is not surprising that the number of ways in which even a common name can be spelt passes belief in both Lancashire and Yorkshire. With some, as we should expect after what we have seen in other counties, variants are due to dispersal of families. Birkenshaw, for example, a West Riding name meaning 'birch wood', has travelled as a surname from Cumbria in the North to Sussex in the South-East and Cornwall in the South-West, acquiring at least twenty-three variants before becoming Brokenshire in Cornwall. But even Birkenshaw was contorted when it moved into Airedale, which is not far from its first home. Cowperthwaite, another West Riding name, became Copperwheat within a few miles of its place of origin.

The -thwaites seem to have been the biggest problem when they were passed on orally from one district to another. Slaithwaite, which means a clearing where sloes grow, is pronounced in any number of ways, including Slewit. Royd, which also means clearing, is almost as big a puzzle, apparently. In Dewsbury records alone there are forty different spellings of Holroyd, and nearly thirty of Ackroyd, a simple name meaning oak-clearing. And not all these variants are attributable to local ignorance or cussedness. The Yorkshireman's pawky humour played more than a minor part in them. I remember an astringent Yorkshire lady who derived great satisfaction from expressing her opinion of a neighbour by always referring to him as Scatterwit instead of Satterthwaite.

The evolution of Industry through cottage crafts, like hand-loom weaving and spinning, contributed greatly to the survival of local dialects in Lancashire, where immigrations from Wales were also an important factor. This shows itself especially in the final 's' in such names as Jones and Williams, and in patronymics from personal names that have gone out of use. Parkinson from Perkin is an example. Ellis, from the now infrequent Elias, is another. But not all of these were the result of immigration from Wales. Some apparently Welsh traits in Lancashire were due to the survival of the British, or Celtic, refugees in the foothills of the Pennines, which Ekwall thought must be 'the explanation of so many British place-names being found there. This is supported ethnologically by the presence of so many small-boned, dark-complexioned families with early surnames derived from personal names in such districts as the fells of Bowland.

These Celtic surnames are curiously regionalised. Jones has been common in Liverpool from an early date, so it cannot be related to the Pennines. It can only be accounted for by Welsh immigration, whereas Roberts, apparently another Welsh name, is strongly localised in the east of the county around Burnley, Padiham, and Colne. As it is also a common name in the West Riding of Yorkshire, the branches of the Roberts family in this part of Lancashire are more likely to be descended from an ancestor who crossed the Pennines out of Yorkshire than from one who came from Wales.

Scotsmen, by contrast, did not reach either Lancashire or Yorkshire in numbers before the Stuarts came to the throne. So names beginning with 'Mac' were rare in Lancashire before the influx of Scottish doctors in the nineteenth century. As they seem to have started in Liverpool, one cannot help wondering whether they originated with the medical men that the law required slaving ships to have on board.

The most striking imported names are those in the Furness area of Lancashire, now part of Cumbria, where families from Germany and the Low Countries brought in to work the copper mines introduced such names as Phemke and Platziner. The number of such immigrants from Flanders was so great that Dr. Leech of Manchester, who examined Lancashire surnames over a long period and published his findings,[1] counted four hundred and three entries for persons named Fleming in the Coniston parish register and three hundred and five in the one for Torver. The land-owning Fleming family were at Coniston Hall from the thirteenth century to the eighteenth, when they made Rydal their principal residence. The name is also common in Pennington and Ulverston. Dr. Leech was yet another writer to express surprise at the number of different ways in which a common name could be spelt in the same parish register; but as there are some very odd place-names in Lancashire we may be less surprised than he was to find Fazakerley, for example, which means 'border strip', spelt in so many ways in the Aughton parish register.

The localisation of surnames, which is still a feature in Lancashire and Yorkshire in contrast to the Midlands, where they circulate freely, applied equally to baptismal names. Higson is a local form of Hickson, in which Hick was a colloquial alternative to Dick. In the same way, Townson is the North Lancashire form of Tomlinson. And localisation of pronunciation applies to names with place-name origin no less than to those with personal-name origin. If you live in the Forest of Bowland you will know that Browsholme is pronounced Broosam. You will not be likely to know this if you live in Stockport, shall we say; but then if you live in Bowland you will not be likely to know that the surname Stopforth is derived from the local pronunciation of Stockport. Gaskell is a local pronunciation of Gaisgill, and so we might go on. Hoyle, for hole, however, is more widely understood in both Lancashire and Yorkshire, where most elderly natives must at some time have heard the phrase: 'Put t'wood i't' hoyle' for 'shut the door'. Perhaps the most common distinguishing characteristic of Yorkshire pronunciation is the substitution of 't' for 'd' already mentioned; but even this is found in North Lancashire in the substitution of 'ett' for 'head' in such names as Birkett, 'the birch covered headland'. A particularly persistent idio-

---

1.   *Trans. Lancs. and Chesh. Antiq. Soc.*, vol. LVIII, 1947

syncracy in Lancashire is the feline pronunciation of 'ow' found at Accrington.

In days when families in a sparsely populated parish might choose the same half dozen baptismal names to add to almost as few surnames generation after generation identification became a problem. So the custom developed of using instead such extended personal names as Tom o' Dick's, or Dick o' Bob's, which might be run on to three or four generations of sires, and presumed knowledge of ancestry only possible in long-settled communities. Sometimes a nickname would be entered in a parish register as an *alias*. And these *aliases* could signify more than might be apparent. An examination of the parish register of Whalley in east Lancashire suggests that they were sometimes used to indicate babes born out of wedlock. For the years 1610 to 1615 there are fifty-nine baptisms entered as *aliases*, only one as illegitimate. For the next three years only one is entered with an *alias*, thirty-six are entered as illegitimate. Had a Puritan succeeded a kindly parson or curate who knew that the child born to an unmarried mother would be cherished in tribal fashion by either grandparents or uncles and aunts and could safely bear their name? In some cases this would undoubtedly be so. In others, if the mother had married after the child was born, and her husband had accepted it as the first member of his own family, a humane parson would be happy to give it the benefit of the husband's name irrespective of any proof of paternity.

Parish registers are not, in fact, as conclusive as evidence of either births or baptisms as they are sometimes thought to be. When a tax on parish register entries was imposed in the eighteenth century, many children were baptised privately in their own homes to evade it. One of my own parson ancestors objected so strongly to the ministrations of the Church being a basis for taxation that he only baptised boys in church, adopting the discrimination—not then illegal!— because boys might need proof of Church of England membership for school or apprenticeship.

An intensive study of the surnames in such a parish as that of Whalley in the fifteenth century might be a very worthwhile exercise. It was a large parish, and its abbey, which figured in the Pilgrimage of Grace, had influence extending over a vast area. In pre-industrial Lancashire the drawing power of such an abbey was comparable to that of East Anglian towns during the Middle Ages. Every village name over a large area surrounding Whalley is now a common surname, which probably originated when an ancestor crossed the moors to find work at the abbey, or serve in one of the abbot's outlying granges. Evidence of this drawing power of abbeys is found in the large proportion of entries in the Subsidy Rolls that have the preposition 'de' in front of the place-name. And this may remind us that some of the proudest records of local families in this part of Lancashire are connected with the Pilgrimage of Grace. There were the Andertons of Euxton, with branches at Horwich, Garstang, Clayton-le-Moors, Colne and other places, who were reported as being county magistrates opposed to the Protestant reforms of 1564. Members of this family figured prominently in religious disputes for several generations. Thomas, Archdeacon of Lancashire, was a secular priest at Townley Hall, Burnley, an eminent Roman Catholic house, from 1705 to 1741.

There were, of course, equally eminent families on the Protestant side during this turbulent period, and some who stood aside. The Lancashire Ormerods were at Ormerod House, Whalley parish, from 1311 to 1793. When we cross the Ribble at Whalley we pass the inn sign 'Judge Walmesley', reminding us that Sir Thomas Walmesley of Dunkenhalgh was a Judge of the Common Pleas in Elizabeth I's reign, and that a kinsman was in Charles II's list of intended Knights of the Royal Oak, along with Thomas Greenhalgh of Read, a Starkie of Huntroyde, and a Shuttleworth of Gawthorpe. The list of such families within a few miles of Whalley could be extended beyond what space would allow here; but the Nowells of Read must be mentioned, and that most respected of long-established families in the district, the pre-Conquest Asshetons of Downham, Lord Clitheroe's family.

In his research into Lancashire surnames Dr. Leech,

whose own name started as a nickname, found that few persons in humble life had surnames before the fifteenth century; but that once they were started they spread rapidly. This is consistent with what others have found about the late adoption of surnames in the North of England, and the persistence of nicknames, many of which eventually became hereditary, for purposes of identification. It was in the late fifteenth century that North Country towns began to expand with increased momentum. The Dissolution meant that new means of employment had to be found, and the towns offered the best field for this. One or two towns were in advance of the trend. As many as seventy *per cent* of those taking part in Preston's Guild celebrations in 1459 had surnames. In 1542 all had them, and occupation names had become prominent with significant variations in both name and meaning. Flecker in regions where there was Scandinavian influence might replace Fletcher as the name of an arrow-maker, and Fletcher could mean butcher, from 'flesher', the name still used in Scotland for the gentleman with the knife and straw hat. In Burnley, basket-makers were called Bannister; Stringers were makers of bowstrings.

In the eighty-four parishes studied by Dr. Leech, the incidence of several occupation-names becomes remarkably revealing. Bowker, for example, was the commonest in Manchester, where Smith came second and Travis third. In many parts of England a bowker was a butcher; but in *Piers Plowman* 'to bouke' meant to wash, and so it did in Lancashire, where a bowker boiled cotton or linen in alkali before bleaching it. The -er was common in Lancashire as elsewhere, even although the adoptions of surnames was so late. One explanation of this is that although surnames were late for those in humble life, the gentry had assumed them in the thirteenth century. The Parker family, which produced a recent Lord Chief Justice and an eminent Lancashire antiquary, have been hereditary Bow-bearers and Keepers of the Forest of Bowland since that time. It is the occupation names in common trades with the -er ending that are most curious. Tyrer is an old Lancashire name from an obsolete word meaning tear or rend. Had this a respectable origin, or was the original Tyrer simply a tear-away? The Nutters were originally neat-herds, or cow-herds, which in Lancashire would be pronounced nowt-herd. Later Nutters were Master Foresters of Trawden Chace and in Elizabeth I's reign a Nutter was Steward of Pendle. Readers of Harrison Ainsworth's *Lancashire Witches* will recall the fame of Mistress Nutter!

A surname for which no-one has yet found a convincing origin is Rimmer. Dr. Reaney says it is from rhymer or rimer. So it may be in some parts; but as it occurs 4,327 times in the Southport parish register, where Smith occurs only 23 times in Dr. Leech's count, we cannot possibly believe that poets or poetasters can ever have been so prolific among the sand dunes. It has been suggested that 'ream' was a local word for a peat bog covered with sand, and that rimmers either lived as squatters in such places or got their livelihood from them. Rim, or edge, seemed to me to be a possible source until I found the name along the Lincolnshire coast and began to suspect that it came from either the Old Norse *hreimr*, or the Dutch *riem*, 'a strip of ox-hide, a thong, a strap', which would make rimmers leather-workers. But I don't know why there were so many of them. Wright's *Dialect Dictionary* gives other possibilities that seem to me to be equally unconvincing. Names peculiar to the vicinity of ports are not, however, unusual. Sleader, which became common at Whitby in the sixteenth century, is believed by the present bearers of the name to have been introduced by fishermen from Germany.

There is no argument about the origin of Spencer, or Spenser, which in any case is not a name confined to the North; but it is interesting because it is common in Lancashire, and because it should not be forgotten that the poet Spenser had Lancashire ancestry. It is also significant because the word 'spence' has continued in use among country folk in the North for pantry, and the word means 'dispenser'. Tennyson used it in *The Talking Oak* for refectory:

> *Bluff Harry broke into the spence*
> *And turn'd the cowls adrift.*

Counting names in these Lancashire parish registers only brings out how settled most of the communities must have been over the long periods required for a small population to become one of many thousands. By the beginning of the present century it was not only in Cheshire that the people were all cousins. Dr. Leech's patient analysis did, however, show how rapidly families must have increased after mid-Lancashire became industrialised. In Rochdale there were so many Butterworths—with Schofields and Cleggs as runners up—that whereas in other parts of England soldiers were called Tommy Atkins, in Lancashire they were called Johnnie Butterworths. In Great Harwood, Hindles, Duckworths, and Howarths (from a Rochdale place-name) were found in nearly every street. Dr. Leech counted 2,275 Hindle entries in the Great Harwood registers, while Fieldings, or Fieldens, and Barons proliferated over the surrounding villages. The Faircloughs, who tended to become Faircloths when they moved South, were in the lead at Wigan, with at least 700 in the parish register at Upholland. The Aspdens and Ainsworths were in strength at Blackburn, with the Dewhursts close behind them. Many of these began as names of manors now forgotten or little known. Catlow, for example, a Clitheroe name, appears first as de Catlowe, the name of a manor in Whalley parish. Duerden, another established name in this part of the county, is derived from Dearden, near Edenfield, Bury. The Tattersalls, strongest in Burnley, owned the Holme estate in Whalley in the fourteenth century, and the Lathams, who derive their name from the Old Scandinavian word for 'barn', were prominent in local government in Lancashire and Cheshire for centuries. Nor must it be forgotten that the Lancashire cotton trade has produced its own honours list, too familiar to be examined here. The Arkwrights and the Cromptons achieved national fame, the former becoming landowners in Essex, while retaining many North Country traits. Some celebrated their pride in having risen from humble origins in their armorial bearings. The family motto of the Shuttleworths, for example, is *Esto Velocior Vita*, 'Be Swifter than Life', an allusion to the flying shuttle. The Pilkingtons, by contrast, did not rise suddenly from humble origins. They held the lordship of the manor of Rivington from 1202 to 1605 and were referred to by Fuller in *The Worthies* as 'a right ancient family'.

Moving north from industrial Lancashire either by way of Preston or the Trough of Bowland to Lancaster and the Lune Valley, we find a greater variety of surnames, which are obviously due to the advantages of this more fertile region for early settlement. Evidence of this is to be seen in the early place-names: Cockerham, Heysham, Tatham (near Torrisholme), a name that takes us along the trail of the Scandinavian settlers. In the fell country of South Lonsdale we have such names as Haythornthwaite, the longest of all the Lancashire surnames, and only two letters shorter than Northumberland's Featherstonehaugh. Not surprisingly, it is corrupted in use to Hathanut. In Lonsdale north of the Sands we find scores of -thwaites, -becks, -riggs, and -ergs—names that can be dealt with more relevantly in Westmorland and Cumberland, and which in Lancashire tend to be found with the final 'g' left out, as in Winder and Torver. But although Winder is the name of parishes in Westmorland and Cumberland, where it means 'a windy pasture', in Lancashire it could be an occupation name for a winder or twister of thread, and although Torver is a place-name it could equally well be the name given to a cutter of turves.

Sturzacre, or Stirzacre, occurs one thousand times in the Garstang parish register, and about one-third of that number of times in that of Preston. It is from a place-name, Stirzacre, and simply means 'steer's or stirk's acre', but it is a rare name seldom found anywhere else—in contrast to Strickland, which has the same meaning and is widely distributed in north Lancashire. One of the -thwaite names that tends to be shortened is Postlethwaite, now sometimes corrupted to Poslett. It means 'the apostle's clearing', and is an example of odd forms taken by Norse names when they drifted south. Postlethwaite became Posselwhite even where attempts were apparently made to keep it uncorrupted, just as Thistlethwaite became Thistlewood, which makes nonsense of the name since thistles grow in clearings and not in woods. In Norfolk, Crosthwaite became Crostwight, suggesting a poor wight crossed in love! Against these peripatetic names are a few that never seem to leave their native heath. Sugden, which means sow-dene, is seldom found outside Yorkshire. But the most 'Yorkshire' of all Yorkshire families are the Metcalfes, whose name probably means 'mead calf' and for that reason is sometimes found as Medcalf. It probably originated as a nickname for a man who appeared to be doing pretty well in life. Even today it is often said in Yorkshire of such a man: 'He looks as though he's brokken into t' meadow'. The Metcalfs of Nappa must have had that appearance in the days of their greatest prosperity. They were so prolific that in 1607 Camden wrote of them that they were counted the most numerous family in England. In 1555, when Sir Christopher Metcalf met the judges at York 'he was attended by three hundred horsemen, all of his own name and kindred, well mounted and suitably attired'.

South Country people tend to think of Lancashire and Yorkshire as completely industrialised. The truth is that they remained rural and sparsely populated in every part until the Industrial Revolution of the nineteenth century, so their surnames are less industrialised than those of most counties and the kind of toponymics found in Devonshire are almost as common in Lancashire and Yorkshire. Many of them provide clues to the pre-industrial landscape. Broadbent, a mid-Lancashire surname, means a wide expanse of coarse grass. Ridehalgh and Greenhalgh incorporate the Northern word 'haugh' for mound or hill. Leach in Lancashire means a boggy stream. Entwistle, which is derived from a place-name, and Birtwhistle, from a lost place-name in Padiham, are derived from an element already discussed: *twisla*, the fork of a river. Raikes, which is from a sheep track—a word found also in Cumbria— belongs to the western side of the Pennines. In Yorkshire a sheep track is more often called a *roddin*, and gives rise to other surnames.

In Yorkshire, swamps and muddy pools in valley bottoms are called dobs. So we get the surnames Dobb and Dobson.

Low-lying land that remains wet most of the year is called carr land. So in the Yorkshire Poll Tax list of 1379 almost every village had someone styled del (of the) Kerr or Carr, descriptions that would become surnames when these were conferred a century or so later. Now, these carrs have been drained, so the word tends to be applied to a low-lying meadow. Snape is a dialect word for winter pasture that survives as a surname. A wham, which meant a grassy hollow or slope, produced the surname Whitwam. Pott in Yorkshire is more likely to be the name of a man who lived near a pothole than of a potter, and yet another word that may have a meaning different from the normal is Grieve. It could mean reeve, in which case Grieveson would be reeve's son; but equally Grieve could be the name given to one who lived near a grove or brushwood thicket. Turning to nationally known names of Yorkshire origin, Asquith incorporates 'wythe' for wood, so is the Yorkshire version of Ashwood, while Thackeray is derived from the corner of a lake where reeds were grown for thatching.

Some of these Lancashire and Yorkshire surnames cannot be said with certainty to have originated in either county separately. The '-shaws' and '-cliffes' belong to both with the -shaws more common in Lancashire and the -cliffes in Yorkshire. Among the former are the Openshaws, Grimshaws, Crashaws (crow-wood), and Earnshaws (either eagle-wood or heron-wood), while the Brayshaws, whose name is a corruption of Bradshaw (broad-shaw), a place-name common in several Northern counties, could be from any of them, although they are now to be regarded as a Lancashire family. The same applies to Wallbank, in which the first element in the name is from a form of 'well' found in the Midlands as well as the North. The 'bank' element suggests that the use of the name was extended to one living on the bank of a stream running from the well or spring that gave rise to the first part of the name. The importance of these wells or springs is shown in the large number of surnames derived from them. They include Aspinwall in Lancashire, and both Haswell and Heswell.

In looking for historical differences that might have

affected surname structures in these two counties, we see at once the relevance of Yorkshire having been over-run by invaders to a far greater extent than Lancashire, and eventually of its Norman domination. Consequently we find surnames arising out of settlement that was not only early but sporadic. Airedale and Wharfedale have many names ending in -ley from Anglian invasion. They include Stanningley, Calverley, Apperley, Keighley, and Bradley in Airedale; Leathley and Burley in Wharfedale. Some of the families bearing these names are still living there, and could probably prove long pedigrees for themselves, particularly as some of them lived on the same farm for hundreds of years. The Calverleys are now dispersed; but they go back to the reign of Edward I.

These Anglian names disappear when we reach Swaledale, where they are replaced by Norse; but in the Craven uplands of the West Riding -ton endings are found in such names as Broughton and Thornton, with Skipton combining the Anglian -ton ending with the Scandinavianised 'Skip' to mean sheep-town.

The 'hunt the letter' game has many penalties and 'return to base' signs when played in Yorkshire. The substitution of 'g' for 'c' has produced Greswell for Creswell, Gawthorne for Cawthorne, Pigburn for Pickburn, and even where the name has preserved its 'c' it may be pronounced as 'g'. Blakeborough is pronounced Blagbrough, and in east Lancashire, Blackburn is pronounced Blagburn in the vernacular. It is difficult to find either rhyme or reason for some of these substitutions even after recognising that most of them arise out of different racial traditions. Instances of a more familiar substitution, that of 'u' for 'i' are found in Rishworth becoming Rushworth as a surname in Bowland, and Riddlesden becoming Ruddlesden. Along a broad belt of the old Lancashire-Yorkshire border, habits of pronunciation are common to both counties; but the Lancashire name Greenhalgh, which is only corrupted to Greenhalch in Lancashire, becomes Greenheld in Yorkshire.

The commonest characteristic of Yorkshire names is that so many of them end in -son. There is no mystery about the reason for this. It came about quite simply because surnames were not adopted by the majority of Yorkshiremen until the fifteenth century, which was the period in which patronymics were very much in vogue. They became almost universal in Wales, where surnames came into use at the same time, for the same reason. The difference between Wales and Yorkshire in this respect is that whereas the Welsh merely either added 's' to the end of the personal name of the father, or 'Ap' to the beginning, the Yorkshiremen added -son in full. FitzWilliam is probably the only patronymic that can be proved to have become hereditary in Yorkshire in the twelfth century. The family trace themselves back to Godfric, a Saxon. In common with other landowners in Yorkshire they took a Norman name in the hope of ingratiating themselves with the new overlords.

If, then, it is no longer sound to argue that the possession of a name ending in 'son' is proof of Yorkshire, or even Northern, ancestry, since there were many such names in the South before the practice was adopted with such vigour in the North, it may be asked whether there is anything about Northern patronymics that is distinctive. Fortunately, there is. It is the incorporation of a pet form of a personal name, like Robinson from Robertson, Dickson or Dixon from Richardson, Wilson from Williamson, Megson from Margaretson, Mallinson from Mary's or Molly's son. And patronymics did not stop with sons in the North. There are instances in South Lancashire of names ending in 'daughter', and Watson, from Walter's son, produced a group of ambiguous surnames that still puzzle scholars. They include Whatmough, Watmuff, Whatmaugh, and other elements that seem to imply a relationship other than that of a child. It could be one drawn in by marriage, such as a son-in-law. My personal guess is that it originated in joint tenures of land which gave advantages to the surviving partner. We shall see in the next chapter how important customary tenures were in the North.

The close personal aspect of relationships in the North is found also in the number of names ending in 'man'. Bateman meant Bartholomew's man; Jackman, Jack's man, and Harriman, Harry's man. In small isolated communities the relationship between man and master was much closer than in populous areas. The servant-man usually lived in the master's house, and not infrequently married one of the master's daughters, to become the master himself in due course. Some of the most respected families in the North started in this way, and many must have started early. The Fentimans, for example, have farmed in the lower Aire valley for six hundred years, and Tesseyman, a name recorded in York in 1283, is still to be found in York and in other Yorkshire towns—which, incidentally is another reminder that although the humbler classes did not acquire hereditary surnames in Yorkshire until the fifteenth century, the gentry had them earlier.

The fertility and persistence of these old Yorkshire families is astonishing, particularly in the remoter dales and on the fells, suggesting that good air and pure spring water were the two overriding factors in promoting healthy stocks. Bradford was to draw its most prolific families from the Bronte country around Haworth, and no doubt other towns could match the experience. The Schofields of Saddleworth are now found in every part of Yorkshire and much of Lancashire. As for the Armitages, whose name curiously enough means hermitage, we can only conclude that few of them can have been celibates. George Redmonds[1] traces the progeny of one John Armitage, who had four sons, thirteen grandsons, one of whom had ten children, and so on until this one branch of the family spread across practically the whole of the West Riding.

But not all families proliferated so vigorously. The Pudseys were lords of the manor of Bolton-by-Bowland from 1349 to 1770, and of these one alone, a fifteenth-century Sir Ralph, had twenty-five children; yet only one Pudsey appears in West Riding directories today, and he may not be a descendant.

In Yorkshire, as everywhere else for that matter, place-names are normally better clues to family origins than

1. *Yorkshire: West Riding.* English Surnames Survey 1, 1973

patronymics, however distinguished. George Redmonds found that well over one hundred place-names in the old parish of Halifax still survived as surnames. The commonest in order of number were Greenwood, Sutcliffe, Holdsworth, Ackroyd, Gledhill, Eastwood, Priestley, Bottomley, Midgley, Woodhead, Illingworth, Barraclough, Helliwell, Crabtree, Horsfall and Lumb. Several of these are duplicated elsewhere, and Greenwood can only have been as common as it undoubtedly was in Yorkshire as the result of family fertility, since there is nothing distinctive about a green wood. Confirmation of its proliferation is found in a statement made by Baring-Gould, that when he went to Horbury Bridge as a curate he found that nearly everybody at Hebden Bridge was called Greenwood. He himself took a wife from another prolific West Riding family, the Taylors, and she bore him fifteen children, fourteen of whom survived. The one name in the Halifax list that does look distinctive is Lumb, since it is a local dialect word for pool.

Have we then disposed of all, or nearly all, the popular beliefs about Yorkshire ancestry? By no means. Nevertheless, when such ancestry has been established, the characteristics that all Yorkshiremen have in common is easily explained. I read recently that a man living today could have as many as half a million ancestors since his surname was first acquired, so it must be quite meaningless in relation to ancestry. The truth is that any man who can trace his family back to the Yorkshire dales or the Pennine fells may rest assured that for the first four hundred years, the ancestors who bore his surname lived in a community where the population was so small and intermarriage so great, that it is not surprising that it should be said that 'you can tell a Yorkshireman anywhere', even if it is cynically added: 'But you can't tell him any*thing*!'

CHAPTER EIGHT
Northern England

Cumbria is a vast expanse in which the names of historic families are as firmly established as the rocks on which their castles and fortified manor houses stand: Lowther, Musgrave, Strickland, Wharton and the rest of them. No less stimulating are the names of their tenants and retainers recorded in such old diaries as those of Lady Anne Clifford, Countess of Dorset, Pembroke, and Montgomery, whose strongholds in the North were at Appleby in Westmorland and Skipton in Yorkshire. Despite the severities of feudalism, the independence that has always characterised the Northerner, based in the Border counties on customary tenure by which property descended automatically from father to son, became so strong that when the Countess raised the rents of her tenant farmers after a long period of stability, they went to law, claiming that these rents had remained unchanged so long that they had now become fixed by custom. Needless to say, they lost and had heavy costs awarded against them.

When the most autocratic of the Lowthers served similar notices on his tenants in the eighteenth century, several families moved into Upper Teesdale in protest; but by that time the case for the landowners had become incontrovertible. The union of England and Scotland had clearly abolished the need to take up arms against invading Scots, which for centuries had been an onerous, if challenging, condition of tenancy. Families in this mountainous region were large and virile. They were, in fact, larger than many of the parish registers indicate. I mentioned in the last chapter how an eighteenth-century ancestor of mine omitted to enter the baptism of girls in his register when such entries became taxable. His attitude had been anticipated by generations of Cumbrian parsons. When the keeping of parish registers became obligatory in 1538, these shrewd North Country parish priests suspected that these entries might be used as a basis for taxation, and tax-gatherers did not rank high in their version of the Gospels. So few parish registers in Westmorland or Cumberland were accurately kept before the beginning of the seventeenth century, and many not even then. Only three in Westmorland—those of Kirkby Lonsdale, Morland, and Lowther—were actually started in 1538. Nevertheless, Sir Bernard Burke was so impressed by the continuity of several of these old Cumbrian families that he commented on the strength of their pedigrees.

In Westmorland the yeomen who gave personality to the countryside they peopled were called 'statesmen'. The name is derived from the 'estates' they held: Addisons, Dents, Fishers, Wilsons, and others who had lived in the same parishes and intermarried for eight hundred years or more. George Washington's ancestors had been among them. Although the name is derived from a place in County Durham, where in 1183 a member of the family acquired the manor from the bishop by service of attending the episcopal hunt with four greyhounds, the President's ancestor emigrated from Dillicar, near Grayrigg, north-east of Kendal in the seventeenth century. The Durham estate had been sold back to the See in 1613.

As we enter Cumbria from Lonsdale we quickly notice such names as Douthwaite, Braithwaite, Summersgill, and others already encountered in Lancashire and Yorkshire. Most of them must have started in Cumbria with Norwegian settlers. Even Schofield is from the Norse *skali*, indicating that the father of all the Lancashire and Yorkshire Schofields settled in a mountain hut. More problematical are the Irish names brought in by the Norwegians, many of which begin with 'Ire'. Coleman, which elsewhere means charcoal burner, in Cumbria may be from the Irish personal name Colman (from Columban), and Brian, which in the South is a Breton name, may be the Old Irish O'Brien. Apparently, this name crossed the Pennines from Cumberland into Yorkshire.

Another ambiguous name is Gill, which in the North is usually from the Irish gaelic *gilla*, meaning servant or gillie, but could have started out as del Gill, and be the name originally given to a man who lived near a glen or ravine. Fothergill (foddering gill) has this derivation, which occurs in so many farm names in Upper Teesdale: Soulgill, Wemmergill, Arngill and so on. In the South of England, it may be corrupted to Gell; but as this is pronounced with a soft 'g' it is probably from a pet name for a long forgotten Gillian. Other names brought over from Ireland by the Norwegians continue as the names of the patron saints of village churches.

Today we think of the North as symbolic of stability and steadfastness; but its history, of course, was turbulent for centuries and left deep-seated divergences. That between Northumberland and Cumberland, which persists to the present time, dates from the collapse of the Northumbrian kingdom and the conquest of northern Cumberland by the Britons of Strathclyde in the 9th century. Evidence of this is still to be seen in the number of British place-names along the Scottish border—except along the Solway, where the Northumbrians were able to hold out from their stronghold at Carlisle. So even now there is as much racial difference between the people of Northumberland and those of Cumberland in the North as there is between the Peoples of Devon and Cornwall in the South-West.

Linguistically the most striking division is between the burns and the becks in the naming of streams. Those that flow into the Tees from Stainmore on both banks are called becks, giving us many surnames with that ending. In Weardale the burns take over and continue northward through Durham and Northumberland to become universal in Scotland, where they gave us the name of the national poet, although water was not his favourite drink. In one place in Teesdale we have Raygill burn, combining the Celtic 'ray' and the Norse 'gill' with 'burn', and in Weardale we get the odd name, Beechburn Beck. Some of these names may have originated with early cartographers giving names to streams that had never had them, and are a warning against the too-literal interpretation of surnames no less than of place-names. Such well-known Northumberland surnames as Milburn and Swinburn clearly indicate their place of origin; but Hebburn, from a place-name in Durham, and Hepburn from one in Northumberland have completely different origins. The 'burn' in them is not from a stream, but from the Old English *byrgen*, 'tumulus', a reminder of the custom of raising mounds of earth to commemorate dead heroes.

Celtic names survive in the mountainous regions of Durham as they do in the Pennines to the south. So we have such names as Stanhope (stony valley) surviving to become surnames, although Anthony Trollope's name, which means 'troll-valley', probably had its origin in 'Trolhop', an earlier name for Troughburn, Northumberland. There are no fewer than sixteen 'hopes' in Weardale. In the lowlands to the east we get a crop of Anglian place-names that became common surnames, with those ending in -ton in such names as Darlington (with -ing incorporated), Haughton, and Stainton, being succeeded in a later period of settlement by place-names with descriptive terminals like -field to produce the Sedgfield group of surnames in Durham as well as the commoner Sedgwick in Westmorland. Scandinavian place-names are rare in Durham; but this does not mean that there were no Scandinavian settlements in the county. It simply means that they were late and only came after the place-names had been established.

Scandinavian influence was certainly strong in Upper Teesdale, where we have several names with Anglo-Saxon endings. Most of them are on the Yorkshire bank of the river and seem to have been on the estate owned by one, Torfin, who took his name from the god Thor. In general, however, as we move across Durham, Scandinavian names give place to Anglian. A count of Scandinavian place-names in Northern England gives 158 in Westmorland, 142 in Cumberland, 23 in Durham, and 22 in Northumberland. This is remarkable when we find over 400 of them in the three Ridings of Yorkshire, where there are 167 -by endings, 95 -thorpe endings, against only 7 of each in Durham and only 1 in Northumberland. When we turn to the -thwaites, which are so common in Westmorland and give rise to a host of surnames, we find that they are absent from Northumberland, and that in Durham there are only a few in the extreme south of the county. The conclusion to be drawn from these figures is that even after the Scandinavians had gained dominance, most of the families continuing to work the land away from the hills were Anglo-Saxon in origin. There is, in fact, abundant evidence of peaceful co-existence in the North Riding of Yorkshire in the way Anglian and Scandinavian place-names, such as Stainton and Stainsby, Thornton and Thornaby, are found side by side, with such surnames established in them as Ingleby, the -by of the English.

Linguistically, the Scandinavian races produced similar names; but as settlers they were sharply divided between Danes and Norwegians. The Danes came in from the east to settle the fertile dales of the North Riding of Yorkshire, or press through the Pennine Gap to settle the eastern fringes of the Lake District, their settlements petering out when they reached the mountains, where Celtic names and ancient earthworks remain from older cultures. It was into these mountain fastnesses that the Norse shepherd stock came by way of Morecambe Bay and the Solway from Ireland to settle regions that held no attraction to the Danes or Angles; but which these races had already encircled.

In these billowing mountain ranges the Norwegians established themselves and built up the traditions of character and austere ways of living that Wordsworth so much admired. In Cumberland they spread out into small existing settlements to produce hybrid names like John Peel's Caldbeck, Redmain, and that most curious of all North Country surnames, Blennerhassett, derived from a combination of the Welsh *Blaen-dre*, 'hill farm', and the Norse 'hay-shieling'. Members of this family represented Carlisle in Parliament continuously from the reign of Richard II to that of James I. But the deep attachment of the Norwegians to the mountains is found in names ending in -erg, -sett, -thwaite, -scale, and -holm, many of which were to become common surnames among their descendants when these were adopted as late as the fifteenth century.

In general, Scandinavian elements in both place-names and surnames are descriptive. In some they crystalise ancient legends of folk heroes. Osmotherley, a name in the North Riding of Yorkshire and a township in Ulverston, means the *leah* of the God-protector. It is corrupted to Osmondy, the local pronunciation of the place-name. Airey, usually found as Airy, is an example of a descriptive name. It appears in 1332 at Threlkeld in Cumberland, with Aira Beck and Aira Force, Ullswater, to the east, and probably means 'gravel-bank' from the Old Norse *eyrará*. So the surname means 'dweller by the gravel-bank'. It is one of many such names in this part of Cumberland. Threlkeld, which is both a place-name and a surname, is not only at the centre of them but is associated with one of the most romantic of all the cherished memories of the North. It was the hiding-place of the children of the Lancastrian 'Butcher Clifford' after the Yorkist victory at Towton. One of these children was reared in a shepherd's cottage, so was known as the 'shepherd lord' until he was restored to his estates and became 'the good Lord Clifford'. His story is told in Wordsworth's poem *The White Doe of Rylstone*. Threlkeld, the place, lies at the foot of Blencathra, which incorporates the Welsh *blaen*, 'hill', and is now called Saddleback. It was one of the three homes of the Threlkeld family, whose other lands and homes at Yanwath and Crosby Ravensworth were held under the Greystokes, who originally held them from the Cliffords. The relationship between these reigning Cumbrian families can often be traced through their armorial bearings, especially in this case through the annulets that appear to have been first incorporated by the Viponts, the original holders of the barony of Westmorland, from whom it passed to the Cliffords.

William Jackson, who did work on the St. Bees parish register for the Cumberland and Westmorland Antiquarian Society's transactions, examined many of these alliances and while doing so brought to light several old names that are now less common than they used to be. Among them is

Woodall, which may have originated in the wood halls in which Forest courts were held. He also drew attention to the local habit of adopting surnames as baptismal names. Dacre was a common one. The assumption of such surnames as personal names by families in humble life might seem presumptuous. It has been suggested that it branded the father of a child born out of wedlock. Young lords did sire children among their tenantry; but these were not flaunted. The most likely explanation is that—apart from cases in which it was the mother's maiden name—in a paternalistic society a kindly employer agreed to act as godfather to a faithful servant's child and allowed it to be given his name. In districts where Scandinavian influence was strong, great importance was attached to the bearing of an honoured name because it was believed that some of the qualities of earlier bearers would be transferred to the new one, and that the child's fortunes would be watched over even by the departed.

Among the commonly recurring names in the St. Bees register were Grindal, Huddlestone, Leybourne, Skelton, Ponsonby, Salkeld, Wybergh, Curwen and Vipont, all borne sooner or later by men who achieved eminence. The last of these is derived from Vieuxpont and is therefore French. Another interesting French name in this part of Cumberland is Orfeur, from *orfèvre*, 'goldsmith', a name that appears at Plumbland early in the fourteenth century, where it was quickly anglicised to Goldsmith; but as usual the parent stock retained the old name. One cannot help suspecting that the name is associated with the search for precious metals which has such a long history in the North. The Orfeurs were a family of consequence who married into the families of Lamplugh (from the Welsh *Llan Plwy*, the church of the parish), Lowther, Colvill, and Swinburn before the last of the male line removed to Scotland in the middle of the eighteenth century. The name appeared to have become extinct with the burial of Elizabeth Orfeur, a widow, at Aspatria in 1793. It had certainly become so rare that when in 1841 a John Orfeur of Norwich wrote to the incumbent of Plumbland to enquire whether there were any

Orfeur monuments in the church or churchyard, he received the reply that there were none. A year later, however, the curate wrote again to say that a moss-covered tombstone bearing the name of William Orfeur, who was buried in 1706, had been deciphered in the churchyard near the chancel door. *Sic transit gloria mundi.*

After the Viponts, perhaps the most eminent of these immigrants were the Mounseys, who were said by Nicolson and Burn in their history of 1777 to have been 'called kings of Patterdale, living as it were in another world, and having no-one near them greater than themselves'. The very name, Patterdale, is a corruption of Patricdale, a name taken from a member of the Mounsey family in the thirteenth century. The Mounseys of Patterdale were a branch of the Norman family whose name is spelt Monceux in Hurstmonceux, Sussex, and who had originated in Monceaux. Descendants continue in the North-West to this day.

If we are searching for the names of families that have the true Cumbrian character stamped on them we cannot do better than look into Quaker records. It was no mere chance that caused the Quaker faith and way of life to find such ready acceptance among families whose tenets in all things were as basic as those of the Howgills, Backhouses, Braithwaites, Burroughs of Underbarrow, Cammes of Camsgill, Fells of Swarthmore, Hubberthornes of Yealand, Lathams, Fothergills, and Bensons of the Fould in Westmorland and of Borrat near Sedbergh: a family that has bred scholars and divines as well as Quaker yeomen for centuries. John Benson was vicar of Grasmere in 1550, and other members of the family have held livings in all the Northern counties, as well as having given Westminster its last abbot and Canterbury an archbishop whose son, A. C. Benson, Master of Magdalene, Cambridge, gave proof of his northern ancestry when he wrote the lines:

> *I would live, if I had my will,*
> *In an old stone grange on a Yorkshire hill.*

To understand the dignity of the lives these Cumbrian statesmen lived we only need to visit Townend, Troutbeck, now National Trust property, which was the home for nearly three hundred years of the Browne family—farmers, antiquaries, men of a proud but simple race, who link us in spirit with the Crackenthorpes of Newbiggin Hall and the Cooksons of Penrith, whose union bred Wordsworth.

If we are looking for ancient lineage among such families we shall find difficulty in spotting one that is not linked with an honoured name either by direct descent or intermarriage. There can be few that do not at some point bring into their family tree the name Curwen, and the Curwens claim descent from the royal houses of both England and Scotland. Their name is derived from Colvend and was formerly spelt Culwen. Like the Lowthers, whose name is from a Norse river-name meaning 'froth', their wealth was derived from the Cumberland coal mines. The Senhouses (seven howes, or hills) also opened up mines and exported the coal from Maryport, which Humphrey Senhouse named after his wife.

These Cumberland mines did more than make their owners rich. Over a long period they were the only means of attracting new blood into this sheep-rearing country to counteract the effects of inbreeding. In the middle of the fourteenth century the Alston silver and lead mines were worked by a German from Cologne named Tillman, who was brought over to manage them. No doubt a few of his countrymen came with him; but it was not until the middle of the sixteenth century, when Thomas Thurland and Daniel Höchstetter brought German miners to Keswick, that the dalesfolk made their resentment publicly known and took up arms against the immigrants after blood-curdling tales about their ruthlessness had been circulated. For a time they had to be lodged on an island in Derwentwater for safety. Eventually, however, Höchstetters, Tullies, Raisleys (originally Ritseler), Steinbergers and their descendants were received into county families.

A name with which we became familiar in the first chapter of this book, Chaloner or Challoner, turns up unexpectedly in the North. It first appears with Thomas Challoner, who after marrying a Yorkshire heiress became a legend in the Northern counties towards the end of the sixteenth century. The story goes that while hunting near Guisborough he noticed that the soil and vegetation were similar to those near alum works in Italy, which he knew were owned by the Pope and worked at enormous profit. At that time alum was used in the manufacture of cloth, and its production from shale quarried in the Cleveland hills by Challoner's quarrymen introduced to the North a lucrative but grim new industry, which, although the site was seized by James I and declared a 'mine royal', continued to flourish until the 1860s, when the opening up of the South Yorkshire coal mines provided cheaper supplies. The method of producing alum had been a secret carefully guarded by the Holy See, and tradition has it that in order to get Yorkshiremen trained, Challoner smuggled workmen from the Pope's mines into England in casks. This so enraged the Pope that he issued a bull cursing Challoner to all eternity in the violent terms which so amused Laurence Sterne that in *Tristram Shandy* he allows Dr. Slop to make a running commentary based on them.

Most of the great families associated with County Durham in the proud days of the prince bishops have now moved out or become extinct: Nevilles, Eures, Conyers, and Hiltons. A few, like the Vanes, Lambtons, and Lumleys, who have been there since the twelfth century, remain. The Crasters of Craster, near Alnwick, have held their estate since the time of Henry I. All these families intermarried, and most if not all derived their wealth from mining. Even the Bowes owed much of their early wealth to their ownership of the lead mines in Teesdale. Other mining families, which are the opposite numbers, as it were, of the great clothier families that brought such wealth to the West of England, include the Blakistons, Bellasises, Claxtons, Hodgsons, Liddells, Lilburnes, Mitfords, and Riddells, many of whom married into the old landed families precisely as the clothier families of the West and the manufacturing families of the Midlands did. In the seventeenth century, for example, Sir Robert Hodgson married Frances Ingleby, a great-granddaughter of the last Neville earl of Westmorland.

Two of the most eminent Durham families followed the custom we found in Wiltshire of taking their title from rivers: the Surtees from the Tees, the Eden from the Eden, and it is interesting to note that when Sir Anthony Eden was made a viscount he again took his title from a river.

Meanwhile the old yeoman families, with their privileged system of tenancy, again invite comparison with the yeomen of Kent, by aspiring to gentility in the eighteenth century, when their pedigrees began to appear in county histories. Durham especially has a wealth of evidence of this from having Surtees as its great historian, and antiquarianism flourishing so long among the clergy. The steady rise in status of both yeoman and clerical families in the Tudor and Stuart periods is examined by Mervyn James in *Family, Lineage, and Civil Society* (1974), a valuable contribution to local history, which brings out the fact that there was a minor industrial and social revolution in Durham during that period. Nevertheless, the clan spirit remained strong, as also did the paternalism of such families as the Whartons, who clearly felt responsible for the moral as well as the economic welfare of their tenants. 'Lord Wharton bibles' continue to be treasured possessions in many Northern households.

Repeating the pattern found in the South and West, the leading family throughout the Middle Ages came into Durham as constables of the castle. Surtees in his *History of Durham* traces the families descended from the Roger Conyers who was appointed to the office by William the Conqueror. There were the Conyers of Hornby Castle, Bowlby, Hutton-Wiske, Thormanby, Pinchinthorpe, Marske, High Dinsdale, Wynyard, Layton, Horden, Coltham, Conyers in Durham and Hopper in Northumberland. Although the name is still common, one by one their landed possessions left them until in 1810 the last of the direct line, Sir Thomas Conyers, would have passed from Chester-le-Street workhouse to a pauper's grave if a subscription list had not been opened to give him a burial more fitting for the last of a proud race that had figured so prominently in the North for nearly eight hundred years. At his death the original baronetcy became extinct. A similar fate befell many of these Norman families. Descendants of Hamon de Clairvaux, whose family was at Croft, near Darlington, for three hundred and fifty years, eventually sank into pauperism.

The decline of other great families has been less dramatic and reflects no discredit on the present holders of historic names. Umfreville was a proud name in Northumberland for centuries after the Conqueror gave the lordship of Redesdale to Robert de Umfreville to hold by service of defending the region 'from wolves and the king's enemies'. The last but one of the line kept a chandler's shop in Newcastle until that also failed and he spent his last years as keeper of St. Nicholas's workhouse there. His son went to sea and became master of a ship; but when he died without issue in 1820, the race expired. In 1880 the name Vipont, spelt Vipond, could be seen on the sign of a grocer's shop at Middleton-in-Teesdale. It continues in the North. The Meynells of Whorlton, north of the Cleveland hills, who came from Mesnil in France, fared better; but they are now dispersed, leaving the fortified village of Whorlton as the great memorial of a wild and romantic tribe.

Purely as a name, the most remarkable in Durham is Featherstonehaugh, which is kept in uncorrupted form. Another outstanding name in the same county was Hansard, which is derived from the Old French word for cutlass, or pomard, suggesting that the original holder was a maker of these weapons in this fighting country. It has been suggested that it means Hanseatic merchant; but Dr. Reaney points out that it appears too early for that origin to be tenable. The Hansards of Evenwood had a seat in the palatinate parliament of the bishops of Durham, and were known as 'the handsome Hansards'.

In Northumberland we get the clan spirit in almost Scottish intensity. The Fenwicks of Stamfordham were the traditional enemies of the Elliotts, the Robsons of the Armstrongs of Liddisdale. The Spearmans, Bowmans, Trewicks and Bewicks were all ready to respond to the bugle call of the Percies. But was it a bugle, or the pipes? Perhaps we should say horn, since the surname Hornblower was formerly found along the Roman Wall. It is a name which could have originated with the man charged to sound the alarm when the Scots invaded, and for doing so held a small estate by serjeanty of cornage, which means the blowing of a horn for such a purpose. Of course, the first Hornblower may have been no more than a town crier; but this is martial country! The Herons, Herrouns and the rest of them derive their name from the nickname given to a man with thin legs. Sir John Hairun, who came in with the Conqueror, held Ford and Chipchase castles, and also Twisell. Sir Walter Scott wrote of him:

> *Sir John the Heron bold,*
> *Baron of Twisell and of Ford,*
> *And Captain of the Hold.*

Other castles were held by the hereditary heads of the families of Swinburn, Behenfield, and Haddeston.

Many surnames spill over into Northumberland from Scotland, which is not surprising, since the Cheviots were neither a linguistic nor a national border while the kingdom of Strathclyde spanned them. Thus Allan, the Scottish form of Allen, is found in Northumberland.

Of the four Border clans in Northumberland the boldest were the Fenwicks. Their name simply means 'dairy farm in the Fen', so is one that might occur in many parts of the country, and not the most likely to be as prominent in border warfare as it was. It was derived in Northumberland from the fens near Stamfordham; but the family always rallied so strongly to the support of the Percies that their battle cry: 'A Fenwick! a Fenwick!' earned them the title of the Fearless Fenwicks. Sir John Fenwick was executed in 1697 after being convicted of plotting the assassination of William III. His confiscated horse, White Sorrell, while being ridden by the king, stumbled on a molehill and is alleged to have been the cause of his rider's death. This gave rise to the Jacobite toast: 'To the little gentleman in black velvet'.

Surnames from the Old Norse, apart from those adopted from place-names, are rarer than we might expect, although

Swayne is one and Clack another. The reason for this is that Scandinavian personal names had virtually become extinct by the time surnames were being assumed and the character-istic -son ending had become common. One name, however, Dring or Dreng, from the Old Norse *drengr*, 'young man', continued in use because it acquired the meaning of 'free tenant', and was used in Northumberland for a young man being granted land by tenure that involved military service.

Church and Army were more closely linked in Durham and Northumberland than elsewhere. The prince bishops had their private armies and military service was usually included in terms of tenancy. But true Christian influences were also strong in this pioneer missionary county. So saint's names became popular, with Cuthbert in the lead pro-ducing Cuthbertson. Several of these names do show Scandinavian influence, and many are localised. Bryce and Bryson are from the St. Britius, or Brice, who succeeded St. Martin as bishop of Tours and was particularly popular in Northern Ireland and Scotland in the twelfth and thirteenth centuries.

The North Country habit of familiarity, which produced pet forms of so many personal names in Yorkshire, continued in Northumberland to produce Robson from Robertson, Kitson from Christopherson, Dawson from Davidson, Lawson from Laurenceson, and Gibson from Gilbertson. This familiarity, which showed itself in adopting pet forms even for saint's names, went so far as to give such names to animals. Every Geordie knows that donkeys and ponies are called Cuddie, the affectionate form of Cuthbert. This is said to have been started by the men who gave the name to favourite donkeys in the trains that carried lead along the pack trails from the mines. The habit is significant. If we are looking for a common factor in the largest proportion of Northern names, we are unlikely to find one more character-istic than this habit of taking disrespectful liberties with personal names when adopting them as surnames.

APPENDIX

A Topographical List of Peculiarly Local Surnames

Abbreviations Bd.—Bedfordshire; Brk.—Berkshire; Ch.—Cheshire; Co.—Cornwall; Ess.—Essex; Gl.—Gloucestershire; Hu.—Huntingdonshire; K.—Kent; La.—Lancashire; Li.—Lincolnshire; Nb.—Northumberland; Nf.—Norfolk; No.—Nottinghamshire; Np.—Northamptonshire; St.—Staffordshire; Sx.—Sussex; Wo.—Worcestershire; Y.—Yorkshire

Bedfordshire
Allingham
Battams
Boteler
Breary
Breed
Breen
Brightman
Bunyan
Dilley
Duncombe
Fensome
Foll
Goodship
Hartop
Infield
Inskip
Marchant
Mossman
Negus
Orlebar
Osborne
Panther
Parish (& Ess.)
Pell
Quenby
Scrivener
Sewell
Timberlake
Titmus

Whinnett
Whitbread
Worboys
Yirrell

Berkshire
Adnams
Ayers
Benning
Bunce
Crockford
Dearlove
Eyston
Freebody
Freelove
Frogley
Froome
Golafre
Halfacre
Izzard
Keep
Kimber
Lowsley
Lyford
Maslen
Norris
Pither
Povey (& Gl.)
Shackell

Buckinghamshire
Belgrove
Brazier
Burnell
Crook
Dancer
Darvell
Dover
Dwight
Ednams
Flitney
Gomm
Goss
Holdom
Ing
Puddiphatt
Purcell
Roads
Slocombe
Tapping
Tofield
Tombs
Tomkins
Vickers
Warr
Wilmer
Wooster

Cambridgeshire
Askew

Beavis
Chivers
Coe
Coles
Collen
Doggett
Elbourne
Ennis
Fowler
Froggatt
Frohock
Haddow
Hagger
Halfpenny
Haylock
Hurrell
Ilett
Ince
Izzard
Jeeps
Murfitt
Norman
Osler
Overhill
Patten
Peppercorn
Purkis
Rayner
Ruston
Sallis
Skeels
Stockdale
Thoday
Vawser
Wayman
Yarrow

Cheshire

Adshead
Allman
Allmark
Ankers
Arderne
Aston
Basford
Basnett

Birtles
Boffey
Bolshaw
Booth
Bracegirdle
Braddock
Brammall (& Y.)
Broadhurst
Broster
Cash
Cassidy
Challinor
Cotterell
Done
Dooley
Furber
Gallimore
Gleave
Hankey
Hickson
Hock
Hollinshed
Hooley
Hopley
Hughes
Jeffs
Jephson
Kenworthy
Kinsey
Leather
Leech
Legh
Littler
Major
Marsland
Massey
Mullock
Newall
Oakes
Okel
Pownall
Rathbone
Ruscoe
Scragg
Shone
Shore
Siddorn

Shufflebottom
Sproston
Tapley
Tickle
Tricket
Venables
Woollam
Worthington
Yarwood

Cornwall

Angove
Angwin
Annlar
Benney
Berriman
Bice
Biddick
Blamey
Boaden
Boase
Bolitho
Borlase
Botterell (& Y.)
Brenton
Budge
Bullivant
Bullmore
Bunt
Burnard
Burt
Cardell
Care
Carew
Carne
Carveth
Cawse
Chenoweth
Clemo(w)
Clymo
Cobbledick
Congdon
Couch
Cowling
Crago
Craze

Crowle	Littlejohn	Trewhells
Cundy	Lobb	Trewin
Curnow	Lory	Tripcony
Dingle	Lugg	Trounson
Dunstan	Lukies	Trudgeon
Eddy	Lyle	Truscott
Eva	Mabty	Tyack
Freeth(y)	Maddaford	Uren
Geach	Magor	Vellenoweth
Geake	Mayne	Venning
Gerry	Moyle	Verran
Gillbard	Mutton	Wichett
Glanville	Oates	Yelland
Glasson	Odgers	
Goldsworthy	Olds	
Grigg	Opie	*Cumbria*
Grose	Pascoe	Addison
Hambley	Pearn	Airy
Hawke	Pethick	Armistead
Hawken	Penaligan	Armitstead
Hearle	Penna	Armstrong
Heilbron	Polkinghorne	Backhouse
Henwood	Prideaux	Benson
Higman	Prisk	Blennerhassett
Hockin	Retallack	Bramwell
Hodge	Roose	Brunskill
Hollow	Roseveare	Burrough(s)
Hosking	Rosewarne	Capstick
Ivey	Roskilly	Cookson
Jago	Rouse	Coulthard
Jane	Rowse	Curran
Jasper	Runnalls	Curwen
Jenkin	Sandercock	Dalzell
Jewel	Sandry	Dent
Jose	Scurrah	Dodgson
Julian	Seccombe	Elbeck
Julyan	Skerratt	Ewbank
Keats	Spargo	Faulder
Kerkin	Tonkin	Fawcett
Kevern	Trebilcock	Fearon
Kitto(w)	Tregoning	Fell
Kneebone	Trelawny	Fleming
Laity	Treleaven	Garnett
Lander	Treloar	Grindal
Lanyon	Trembath	Hetherington
Lean	Trerise	Hogarth
Liddicoat	Treweeke	Hogg

Howgill
Huddleston
Lewthwaite
Mounsey
Musgrave
Nicholson
Patterson
Pattinson
Ritson
Routledge
Senhouse
Slack
Strickland
Tod
Todhunter
Tomlinson
Tunstall
Tyson
Vipont
Woodall
Wybergh

Derbyshire

Babbington
Barke
Beardsley
Boam
Bowmer
Bretton
Byard
Chadfield
Clewes
Copeland
Copestake
Cutts
Drabble
Eley
Else
Eyre
Fearn
Fitchett
Foulkes
Fretwell
Gent
Gratton
Hurt

Jerram
Joule
Longden
Lynam
Maskery
Oakden
Ollershaw
Pegg(e)
Pursglove
Ravenshaw
Revill
Seal
Shawcross
Smedley
Staniforth
Stoppard
Storer
Tagg
Towndrow
Turgoose
Udall
Wallwin

Devonshire

Addems
Aggett
Amery
Anning
Arscott
Babbage
Balkwill
Balsdon
Bater
Bawden
Beedell
Besley
Blatchford
Bolt
Boundy
Braund
Brimacombe
Bucknell
Buddle
Burgoyne
Cawsey
Chaffe

Chamings
Channing
Chave
Chown
Chubb
Chugg
Cleverdon
Coombe(s)
Copp
Courtenay
Courtier
Crang
Crimp
Crober
Cuber
Cudlip
Cudmore
Cuming(s)
Dallyn
Darch
Dare
Dayman
Dayment
Densham
Doidge
Dommett
Drake
Dufty
Dymond
Ellicott
Elston
Endicott
Eveleigh
Fairchild
Faulkner
Fewings
Floyd
Foale
Foss
Friend
Furze
Gammon
German
Gidley
Gilbert
Gillard
Gloyn

Gorrell	Nosworthy	Tooze
Gorwyn	Oldreive	Tozer
Gribble	Paddon	Tremlett
Halse	Palfrey	Trott
Hamlyn	Palk	Trude
Hannaford	Parkhouse	Tucker
Hartnell	Pavey	Tuckett
Haye	Pearcey	Tully
Heddon	Penwarden	Tupper
Heggadon	Perkins	Twitchen
Helmer	Perrin	Underhay
Hext	Petherick	Underhill
Heywood	Pomeroy	Vanstone
Hockridge	Prettyjohn	Voaden
Honeywill	Pring	Vooght
Hookway	Pugsley	Wadland
Hurrell	Pym	Waycott
Huxham	Quance	Yard
Huxtable	Quick	Yeo
Kerslake	Rabjohns	Youldon
Kingwell	Raymont	
Knapman	Reddaway	
Lambshead	Reddicliffe	*Dorset*
Langmead	Retter	Antell
Langworthy	Rew	Atwood
Lear	Ridd	Bascombe
Lerwill	Routley	Bastable
Lethbridge	Ruddle	Benjafield
Letheren	Seldon	Bessent
Lillicrap	Sellek(ick)	Bowditch
Littlejohns	Sercombe	Brickell
Loosemoor	Seward	Brine
Loveridge	Shapland	Budden
Lovering	Sharland	Bugg
Luxton	Sherrell	Bugler
Madge	Slader	Burge
Maunder	Slee	Burridge
Melhuish	Sluggett	Caines
Metherell	Smale	Chilcot
Mildon	Smallridge	Clavell
Mogford	Soby	Cluett
Mudge	Squance	Coombes
Nankivell	Stidston	Crabb
Netherway	Stoneman	Crocker
Newcombe	Tancock	Dorey
Norrish	Taverner	D'Urberville
Northmore	Toms	Freke

Guppy
Hann
Hansford
Hardy
Hollis
Honeyfield
Hooper
Hounsell
Jesty
Kellaway
Larcombe
Legg
Martyn
Mayo
Meaden
Meatyard
Meech
Moyne
Rabbetts
Rideout
Rossiter
Samways
Scutt
Sprake
Strode
Symes
Topp
Tranter
Tuffin
Turberville
Weld
Wrixon
Zebedee

Durham

Allison
Balmer
Batey
Batty
Beadle
Bertram
Blenkinson
Bulman
Bulmer
Burdon
Callender

Chaytor
Cradock
Craggs
Craig
Davison
Eden
Emerson
Fawcett
Forster
Gibson
Greenwell
Hewitson
Hilton
Longstaff
Maddison
Makepeace
Marley
Ord
Pease
Pemberton
Place
Pollard
Proud
Pybus
Raine
Robson
Shotton
Stephenson
Surtees
Tinkler

Essex

Abell (& K.)
Archer
Audley
Aylett
Ayloffe
Ball
Bonner
Brinson
Cant
Capel
Challis
Cramphorn
Cure

Daybell
Dethwright
Dowsett
Eve
Everard
Fairhead
Fanshaw
Godsave
Goodchild
Gowlett
Haddock
Harsnett
Joscelyn
Josselin
Keddy
Kemsley
Kettley
Laws
Leppingwell
Lucking
Marriage
Metson
Mildmay
Mott
Muggleston
Musset
Nottage
Parish (& Bd.)
Paycocke
Poyntz
Pynchon
Quarles
Rainbird
Rebow
Rickward
Ridley
Savill
Sayer
Scruby
Sorrell
Spurgeon
Stonard
Strutt
Sworder
Tredgett
Vaisey
Wainwright

Wakeling
Wiseman

Gloucestershire
Ablett
Annetts
Ballinger
Bartlett
Baskerville
Bassett
Belcher
Bellows
Bubb
Cadle
Camm
Clutterbuck
Comelay
Croome
Cullimore
Drewett
Drinkwater
Fluck
Fortey
Garne
Gazzard
Godsell
Goscombe
Goulding
Hatherall
Hewer
Hignell
Holder
Hyatt
Iles
Knapp
Limbrick
Lusty
Maddock
Minett
New
Niblett
Organ
Parslow
Partridge
Pegler
Pensom(n)

Playne
Povey (& Brk.)
Radway
Ricketts
Rudder
Rugman
Rymer
Sheppard
Shield(s)
Shill
Shipp
Shipway
Staite
Stinchcombe
Theyer
Till
Timbrell
Trotman
Tuffley
Vick
Vimpany
Voyce
Wadley
Werrett
Wintle
Wintour
Witchell
Yeend

Hampshire
Abbinett
Amey
Annett
Attrill
Ayles
Barfoot
Baring
Blackman
Brigg
Budd
Clift
Cobden
Coote
Drewitt
Drudge
Edney

Fay
Finnemore
Fitt
Flux
Gauntlett
Glasspool
Goater
Godden
Goff(e)
Goodall
Goodenough
Gould
Hickman
Jolliffe
Lines
Mardment
Mew
Moggs
Oglander
Paulet
Pew
Poore
Porcell
Pothecary
Punchardon
Purchas
Seaward
Stares
Stride
Turvill
Twitchen
Whitcher
Witt

Herefordshire
Allcock
Banfield
Baskerville
Berrow
Blount
Bowen
Bromage
Callow
Caswell
Croft
Eckley

Embrey
Godsall
Godsell
Hancorn
Harley
Hartshorne
Hobby
Hoddell
Kyrle
Maddy
Mailes
Mainwaring
Marfell
Meadmore
Mortimer
Oakley
Orgee
Pantall
Scudamore
Sirrell
Skerrett
Skyrme
Tudge
Went

Hertfordshire
Batchelor
Bavin
Bonfield
Brett
Cakebread
Campkin
Chalkley
Dellow
Emerson
Gillett
Hankin
Hoy
Ivory
Living(s)
Lock
Mardell
Orchard
Parkin
Puddifoot
Sears

Titmus
Vyse

Huntingdonshire
Bates
Blanchard
Boyall
Cheney
Corney
Coulson
Dabbs
Ekins (& Np.)
Jellis
Ladds
Lenton
Lilley
Looker
Mash
Speechley
Spriggs
Tebbutt

Kent
Abell (& Ess.)
Baldock
Ballard
Belsey
Bing
Boorman
Boulden
Bowra
Brice
Brooker
Buss
Cartier
Chantler
Chiesman
Claridge
Clinch
Coultrip
Coveney
Cowdray
Coyfe
Crittall
Croucher
Curling

Dering
Digg(es)
Dilnot
Dungey
Durtnell
Everest
Fagg
File(s)
Filmer
Fremlin
Furzer
Godden
Goodhew
Hambrook
Hasted
Hatcher
Heath
Hickmott
Hillier
Hogben
Ide (& Sx.)
Inge
Jarrett
Jessup
Kelsey
Knatchbull
Lade
Laslett
Leney
Luck
Maxted
Minet
Minter
Miskin
Morphett
Neame
Nethersole
Orpin
Ovendon
Pilcher
Prebble
Quested
Rigden
Salter
Scoones
Seath
Shirley (& St.)

Sinnock(s)
Snooks
Solly
Stace
Stickells
Stickle
Stroud
Strudwick
Stupples
Style(s)
Swaffer
Tassell
Thirkell
Thirkettle
Tickner
Tomkins
Tomsett
Tuff
Unicombe
Usherwood
Vinson
Wacher
Weller
Whatman
Wickenden
Witherden
Wyles

Lancashire

Alker
Alty
Assheton
Bent
Bleazard
Bulcock
Catlow
Charnley
Clifton
Collinge
Crashaw
Crompton
Cronshaw
Cunliffe
Duerden
Dewhurst
Duckworth

Duxbury
Eastham
Entwistle
Fairclough
Fazackerley
Forshaw
Gornall
Gregson
Grimshaw
Hardacre
Haworth (& Y.)
Haydock
Hayhurst
Haythornthwaite
Heap
Hesketh
Hesmondhalgh
Higson
Hindle
Holden
Horrocks
Kay
Kenyon
Knowles
Lever
Livesey
Longworth
Lyon
Margerison
Marshland
Mashiter
Maudesley
Nowell
Nuttall
Nutter
Ormerod
Postlethwaite
Ramsbottom
Rawcliffe
Rimmer
Sagar
Seddon
Sephton
Sharples
Shorrock
Southworth
Sowerbutts

Stirzacre
Swarbrick
Thistleton
Towneley
Townson
Trappes-Lomax
Tunnicliffe
Walmesley
Walsh
Wareing
Westhead
Whipp
Whitaker
Whiteside
Winder
Windle
Winkley
Woolton
Worsley

Leicestershire
& Rutland

Barnacle
Berridge
Betteridge
Bibby
Branson
Buckmaster
Cobley
Cokinbred
Dexter
Draycott
Eames
Forryan
Frearson
Geary
Gimson
Glenn
Henson
Herrick
Heyrick
Hornyold
Leadbetter
Lester
Macauley
Maccley

Mold
Musson
Orton
Paget
Pawley
Purefoy
Randolf
Randull
Shipman
Skeffington
Toone
Tugby
Vann

Lincolnshire
Aldis
Anketell
Beck
Blades
Blankley
Borman
Bowser
Butters
Cammack
Codd
Colcheeper
Cutforth
Dannatt(ett)
Dimbleby
Dook
Dowse
Dring (& Nb.)
Ducker
Duckering
Dudding
Elvidge
Evison
Forman
Frisby
Frow
Gaunt
Gilliatt
Goodyear
Gunnis
Herring
Hewson

Ingall
Jolland
Leggett
Lilley
Marfleet
Markham
Mastin
Maw
Mawer
Minto
Palethorpe
Patchett
Pickwell
Riggall
Rippin
Scrimshaw
Westaby

Norfolk
Abbs
Aldous
Amies
Attoe(how)
Bacon
Beck
Bettinson
Bird
Blyth
Boddy
Bond
Brasnett
Brisley
Bundy
Buxton
Cannell
Casson
Catchpole
Cattermole
Causton
Cavell
Cawston
Coe
Colby
Colman
Conisford
Coxford

Cranworth
Crowe
Cubitt
Curson
Dalling
Denver
Docking
Dyball
Dyce
Eglinton
Flatt
Foulsham
Fountain
Frere
Gallant
Gamble
Gapp
Gaywood
Gaze
Gedge
Girling
Gissing
Gooderston
Goose
Goulder
Gresham
Gunton
Gurney
Hack
Hackett (& Wo.)
Hackford
Hardingham
Hawes
Hayward
Helsdon
Horsford
Howard
Howe
Huggins
Jarmy
Jarrold
Jermy
Joicey
Kelling
Kerridge
Kerrison
Lammas

Larwood
Leeder
Lenn
Mack
Marsham
Milk
Mountford
Mumford
Mundford
Narborough
Negus
Nurse
Pegrum
Purdy
Rainbird
Ralph
Reader
Reeder
Ringer
Rivett
Rolph
Sallis
Scales
Sharman
Sheldrake
Shreeve
Slipper
Stimson
Thacker
Thirkettle
Thirtle
Threadgold
Thrower
Tooley
Tuck
Tuttle
Utting
Warner
Whalebelly
Wyndham
and many
ending in
-is and -us

Northamptonshire
Aris
Bazeley

Britten(ain)
Butlin
Cottingham
Daintry(ey)
Drage
Ekins (& Hu.)
Gibbard
Goff
Golby
Gulliver
Hales
Heygate
Isom
Issom
Linnell
Mabbett (etc.)
Mackaness
Main
Mawby
Newitt
Orlebar
Panther
Passell
Passingham
Pateshall
Roddis
Scrivener
Spokes
Stops
Turnell
Waldegrave
Walgrove
Weldon
Wrighton

Northumberland
Ainsley
Alder
Alderson
Allan
Anderson
Annett
Armstrong
Aynsley
Bainbridge (& Y.)
Bewick
Blenkinsopp

Borthwick
Bowman
Bryce
Bryson
Carmichael
Christie
Craster
Crawford
Cuthbertson
Dawson
Ditchburn
Dring (& Li.)
Earle
Embleton
Ewart
Fairbairn
Fairlamb
Fairless
Featherstone
Featherstonehaugh
Fenwick
Gilhespie
Glendenning
Grey
Grieves
Heddon
Henshaw
Hepburn
Hetherington
Hodgson
Hogg
Ilderton
Ingram
Killingworth
Kirsopp
Kirton
Lawson
Liddell
Liddle
Lumsden
Milburn
Mitford
Ogle
Ord
Ormston
Percy
Pringle

Reaveley
Ridley
Ridsdale
Rowbery
Shafto
Spearman
Stamfordham
Steel
Stobart
Swinburn
Telfer
Telford
Thirlwell
Trewhitt (etc.)
Trewick
Turnbull
Usher
Wanless
Weddell
Wedderburn
Whittingham
Widdrington
Younger

Nottinghamshire
Ainsley
Annable
Arnold
Attenborough
Bartram
Basford
Beardall
Beecroft
Billyard
Blatherwick
Blye
Blythe
Broadberry
Budgeford
Carver
Challand
Chettle
Cockin
Collick
Cotgrove
Cottam (& Y.)

Cromwell
Esam
Footitt
Gilsthorpe
Grummitt
Gunn
Hardstaff
Howitt
Hucknall
Huskinson
Keyworth
Kneeshaw
Langford
Limby
Markham
Nott
Oldknow
Paling
Paulson
Peatfield
Pell
Plumtre
Poulter
Quebell
Scrooby
Staples
Stubbins
Truswell
Tuxford
Weightman
Yapp

Oxfordshire
Akers
Arnatt
Astall
Batts
Benson
Bodycoat
Chaundy
Clack
Ensom
Florey
Gilkes
Hambro
Hobley

Hutt
Instone
Jukes
Loosley
Louch
Lovegrove
Luckett
Medley
Neighbour
Noke
Overy
Paxman
Pether
Shrimpton
Spilsbury
Tew
Turry
Whitney

Shropshire
Bebb
Beddoes
Bennion
Benthall
Binyon
Botfield
Bowdler
Breakwell
Brisbourne
Cadwallader
Chetwynd
Cleeton
Corbet
Corfield
Cureton
Duce
Eddowes
Everall
Gatacre
Grindal
Growcott
Gwilt
Hickford
Heighway
Hoddinot
Hotchkiss

Inions
Ledwidge
Madocks
Mellings
Millchamp
Minton
Nickem
Nickless
Onions
Pickford
Pitchforth
Plowden
Puleston
Walwyn

Somerset
Antill
Aplin
Arundale
Arundel
Ashman
Attwell
Baber
Badman
Bagg
Batt
Bicknell
Biddle
Bignell
Bignold
Binning
Bisdu
Board
Bowering
Buddle
Bumble
Burch
Burston
Bythsea
Cary
Case
Chew
Clapp
Clothier
Clouter
Coate

Cogan
Comer
Corp
Cory
Counsell
Creed
Croome
Crosse
Crossman
Curry
Dallimore
Dampier
Denman
Derrick
Dibble
Dicks
Diment
Durston
Dyke
Embery
Evershed
Fanner
Farthing
Fear
Floyd
Fortescue
Gane
Genge
Giblett
Greed
Haggett
Hatch
Hebditch
Hembrow
Hoddinott
Horder
Horsey
Huggler
Hurd
Hurley
Ilett
Isgar
Keen
Kiddler
Kidwell
Lippiatt
Look

Lovibond
Loxton
Lucott
Luttrell
Maggs
Maidment
Malet
Mapstone
Meaker
Oram
Padfield
Parret
Perham
Pether
Petherham
Phippen
Pitman
Popham
Pople
Pottenger
Potticary
Pow
Puddy
Pullen
Rawle
Reakes
Rood
Rugg
Satchell
Say
Sealey
Sellwood
Singer
Slade
Slocombe
Speed
Sperring
Spratt
Stallard
Stawell
Steeds
Stuckey
Summerhayes
Swanton
Sweet
Tanton
Tarr

Tatchell
Tazewell
Teek
Tilley
Toogood
Tosewell
Tozer
Tucker
Tyley
Vanner
Vigar
Vowles
Westcott
Winslade
Winstone
Withers
Withey
Wookey
Wyatt
Yandell
Yeandle

Staffordshire

Aldridge
Armitage
Ashley
Audley
Baddeley
Baggaley
Bagnall
Bagnell
Bagnold
Baskeyfield
Batkin
Beardmore
Bickerton
Biddulph
Bloor
Boden
Bott
Boulton
Bowers
Bowler
Branson
Bronson
Brunt
Bryan

Cadman
Cantrell
Chell
Clewlow
Clowes
Colclough
Colley
Corbishley
Coven
Cumberbatch
Cumberledge
Crump
Danks
Deakin
Deeley
Doxey
Durose
Eardley
Elsmore
Farrall
Fearn(s)
Fernyhough
Forrester
Fosbrooke
Gadd
Goldstraw
Grindley
Haden
Hammersley
Hanley
Heler
Henshall(w)
Hewitt
Hodgkins
Hollins
Homer
Howson
Jeavons
Keeling
Kidd
Knightley
Lakin
Leese
Leighton
Limer
Lindop
Lovatt

Lovenbury
Lymer
Malkin
Marson
Mayer
Mottram
Mugglestone
Myatt
Orpe
Oxley
Parton
Pyatt
Rawsthorne
Rudyard
Sheldon
Shenstone
Shenton
Shirley (& K.)
Shufflebotham
Stoddart
Swetnam
Swynnerton
Tibbett
Tinsley
Tomkinson
Torr
Truscott
Tunnicliffe
Turnock
Warrilow
Willis
Wilshaw
Woodhouse
Woodings
Woolescroft
Wrottesley

Suffolk

Aldous
Aspell
Aves
Basham
Blowers
Boatwright
Boggis
Borrett
Bradley

Brandon
Braytham
Button
Candish
Canham
Catchpole
Cattermole
Challis
Clare
Cobbold
Cracknell
Cressy
Cutting
D'Aeth
Deadman
D'Eath
Dunnage
Erswell
Finbow
Gandy
Gaselee
Girling
Gomme
Grimwade
Haylock
Hayward
Hilder
Isworth
Jarrold
Joysey
Kearsey
Kerrick
Kerridge
Ketteridge
Lewington
Lidgate
Pagnam
Peasnall
Prettyman
Rignell
Ruggles
Sheldrake
Soames
Squirrell
Stannard
Steward
Steggall

Thurman
Tollemache
Tremwade
Trillo
Vesey
Wansey
Watcham
Windus

Surrey

Bodley
Burston
Caesar
Chaundler
Chitty
Chuter
Furlonger
Godleman
Gosden
Hackman
Lewry
Micklem
Mortlock
Peyto
Putnam
Puttock
Ropley
Shorter
Smithers
Tice
Tolwith
Wapshott

Sussex

Akehurst
Allcorn
Ashling
Ayling
Aylwin
Bartelot
Bax
Bedser
Birling
Bloomer
Bodle
Bonniface

Bossom
Botting
Bourner
Broadbridge
Burrell
Cawley
Challen
Chitty
Clarridge
Coppard
Corke
Cornford
Courthope
Crowhurst
Culpepper
Diplock
Downes
Dumbrill
Durand
Eridge
Etheridge
Evershed
Fagg
Fellick
Fogden
Funnell
Furzer
Gander
Goacher
Goring
Gorridge
Gotobed
Gratwick
Haffenden
Hatcher
Head
Henty
Hoad
Hoather
Hobden
Hogben
Honeysett
Hyling
Ide (& K.)
Isted
Killick
Langmead

Leppard
Lewknor
Message
Mounfield
Mountfield
Packham
Pallant
Pankhurst
Penfold
Pilbeam
Pluckrose
Rapley
Ridge
Rivers
Sayers
Sinden
Stapley
Streeter
Stubber
Suter
Tester
Tobitt
Tribe
Verrall
Walder
Waldron
Wickens
Wickers
Woodhams
Wren

Warwickshire

Ansley
Arch
Arden
Brinkler
Brinklow
Brocklehurst
Burbridge
Burman
Chattaway
Chivers
Clancy
Crofts
Dunning
Edkins
Grimes

Hickin
Higgins
Jephcott
Keyte
Knibbs
Ladbrooke
Littleworth
Lucy
Moxon
Packwood
Paget
Pettifer
Stratford
Tapp
Truelove
Truslove
Tunnicliffe
Verney
Weetman
Willday
Wolston
Woodward

Wiltshire

Awdry
Axford
Baverstock
Beake
Bissett
Blunsden
Blunsdon
Bonham
Brinkworth
Bulford
Burbage
Caldicott
Chalcot
Chute
Clarendon
Cotterell
Cottle
Dan
Dancy
Dansey
Dauntsey
Deverell
Draycot

Durnford
Earwaker
Edington
Farleigh
Follitt
Foolé
Francombe
Frankham
Franklin
Freegard
Freeth
Ghey
Goddard
Greenaway
Greenhill
Grist
Gunner
Gurston
Harding
Howse
Hulbert
Hursted
Jupe
Keevil
Kellaway
Kinch
Manners
Musselwhite
Newth
Ody
Ogbourne
Ogburn
Pickett
Pinkney
Pipard
Rowde
Sherston
Thynne
Tidcombe
Tisbury
Titcombe
Wicksted

Worcestershire

Abberley
Abley
Allbutt

Amphlett
Barrett
Blakeway
Byrd
Careless
Cartridge
Doolittle
Eckington
Elgar
Firkins
Foley
Follows
Gabb
Ganderton
Hackett (& Nf.)
Hanbury
Hancock(x)
Hanks
Hemming
Hingley
Holtom
Honeybourne
Honeybun
Kerswell
Mayers
Mayo
Mence
Merrell
Moule
Munn
Newey
Nickless
Pardoe
Penrice
Purser
Quigley
Quinney
Smithin
Spiers
Stinton
Sully
Tandy
Tansell
Timblick
Tipping
Tolley
Westmacott

Willetts
Winnall
Winwood
Yarnold
and names
ending in
-en

Yorkshire
Abdale
Ackworth
Agar
Ambler
Askin
Asquith
Aytoun
Bainbridge (& Nb.)
Bainton
Bairstow
Balby
Bamforth
Barge
Barraclough
Barthorpe
Batty
Beardsall
Beckwith
Beever
Binns
Birkenshaw
Birstall
Blackwood
Blakey
Bland
Boothroyd
Botterell (& Co.)
Bottomley
Brammall (& Ch.)
Branwell
Brearton
Brierley
Brigham
Brotherton
Burlington
Calverley
Calvert
Capstick

Carr
Cockshutt
Cottam (& No.)
Coulton
Cozens
Cudworth
Cundall
Cuttle
Demain
Dent
Dobbs
Dobson
Douthwaite
Dyson
Earnshaw
Embley
Emmott
Eshelby
Feather
Firth
Fossett
Fothergill
Foxton
Frankland
Franklin
Garbutt
Geldard
Gilling
Gledhill
Goodall
Granger
Haigh
Hainsworth
Hancock
Hanson
Hardcastle
Harland
Harrop
Hawksworth
Haworth (& La.)
Hebblethwaite
Hemingway
Hepplewhite
Heseltine
Hinchcliffe
Hodder
Holden

Holdsworth	Moorhouse	Tennyson
Holgate	Murgatroyd	Thornber
Holliday	Oglethorpe	Thwaites
Holroyd	Osmotherley	Tickell
Holtby	Postgate	Tinker
Horsforth	Raistrick	Tunnicliffe
Hotham	Ransley	Umbleby
Hoyle	Rawnsley	Uttley
Huggett	Rotheray	Wadsworth
Illingworth	Rowntree	Weatherhead
Iveson	Sandall	Wentworth
Kearton	Scholes	Widdop
Kinsley	Shackleton	Wilberforce
Kipling	Shillito	Womersley
Lofthouse	Shorrock	Wordsworth
Mallinson	Simpson	Wortley
Marr	Sugden	Wycliffe
Metcalfe	Sutcliffe	
Midgley	Sykes	

Bibliography

BARBER, HENRY; *British Family Names and their Origin and Meaning*, Elliot Stock, 1902

BARDSLEY, C. W.; *English Surnames, their Sources and Significations* (1884), reprint, David & Charles, Newton Abbot, 1969

BARDSLEY, C. W.; *A Dictionary of English and Welsh Surnames*, Chatto & Windus, 1901

BARFIELD, OWEN; *History in English Words*, Faber & Faber, 1962

BARING-GOULD, S.; *Family Names and their Story*, Seeley & Co., 1910

BELDEN, ALBERT; *What is Your Name?*, Epworth Press, 1936

BOWMAN, W. D.; *What is Your Surname?*, Faber & Faber, 1932

BOWMAN, W. D.; *The Story of Surnames*, Routledge, 1932

CAMDEN, WILLIAM; *Remaines Concerning Britaine* (1605) E. P. Publishers, 1974

COTTLE, A. B.; *The Penguin Dictionary of Surnames*, Penguin Books, Harmondsworth, 1967

DOLAN, J. R.; *English Ancestral Names*, London, 1972

DUNKLING, LESLIE; *The Guinness Book of Names*, 1974

DYSON, T.; *Place-Names and Surnames*, Huddersfield, 1944

EWEN, C. L'ESTRANGE; *History of British Surnames*, Kegan Paul, 1931

EWEN, C. L'ESTRANGE; *A Guide to the Origin of British Surnames*, Kegan Paul, 1938

FERGUSON, ROBERT; *Surnames as a Science*, Routledge, 1884

FRANKLYN, JULIAN; *A Dictionary of Nicknames*, British Book Centre, 1962

GUPPY, HENRY B.; *Homes of Family Names in Great Britain*, Harrison, London, 1890

HARRISON, H.; *Surnames of the United Kingdom*, London, 1912–18

HASSALL, W. O.; *History through Surnames*, Oxford University Press, 1967

HOSKINS, W. G., AND FINBERG, H. P.; *Devonshire Studies*, Jonathan Cape, 1952

HOSKINS, W. G.; *The Midland Peasant*, Macmillan, 1957

HOSKINS, W. G.; *Provincial England*, Macmillan, 1963

HUGHES, J. P.; *Your Book of Surnames*, Faber & Faber, 1967

JAMES, MERVYN; *Family, Lineage, and Civil Society*, Oxford, 1974

LATHAM, EDWARD; *A Dictionary of Names, Nicknames and Surnames*, Routledge, 1904

LEECH, E. B.; 'Surnames in Lancashire', *Trans. Lancs. and Chesh. Antiq.-Soc.*, vol. LVIII, Manchester, 1947

LLOYD, L. C.; *The Origins of Some Anglo-Norman Families*, Harleian Society, 1951

LOWER, M. A.; *A Dictionary of the Family Names of the United Kingdom*, Russell Smith, 1860

LOWER, M. A.; *English Surnames: an essay on Family Nomenclature*, Russell Smith, 1875

MATTHEWS, C. M.; *English Surnames*, Weidenfeld & Nicolson, 1966

MCKINLEY, R. A.; *Norfolk Surnames in the Sixteenth Century*, Leicester, 1969

MCKINLEY, R. A.; *English Surnames: Norfolk and Suffolk*, Phillimore, Chichester, 1975

MUNCEY, R. W.; *The Romance of Parish Registers*, Williams, Lincoln, 1933

PAWLEY, WHITE G.; *A Handbook of Cornish Surnames*, London, 1972

PINE, L. G.; *They Came with the Conqueror*, Evans, 1954

PINE, L. G.; *The Story of Surnames*, reprint, David & Charles, Newton Abbot, 1965

REANEY, P. H.; *A Dictionary of British Surnames*, Routledge & Kegan Paul, 1961

REANEY, P. H.; *The Origin of English Surnames*, Routledge & Kegan Paul, 1969

REDMONDS, GEORGE; *English Surnames: Yorkshire, West Riding*, Phillimore, Chichester, 1973

ROUND, J. HORACE; *Family Origins*, Constable, 1930

SMITH, C. ELSDON; *The Story of Our Names*, New York, 1950

STENTON, SIR FRANK; *Anglo-Saxon England*, Oxford, 1943

THOMAS, T. R.; *A Catalogue of British Family Histories*, 3rd edition, Society of Genealogists, 1976

WAGNER, SIR ANTHONY; *English Genealogy*, Oxford, 1972

WEEKLEY, ERNEST; *Romance of Names*, John Murray, 1922

WEEKLEY, ERNEST; *Surnames*, John Murray, 1936

Index

INDEX